Marketing Analytics

Marketing Analytics provides guidelines in the application of statistics using IBM SPSS Statistics Software (SPSS) for students and professionals using quantitative methods in marketing and consumer behavior. With simple language and a practical, screenshot-led approach, the book presents 11 multivariate techniques and the steps required to perform the analysis.

Each chapter contains a brief description of the technique, followed by the possible marketing research applications. One of these applications is then used in detail to illustrate its applicability in a research context, including the needed SPSS commands and illustrations. Each chapter also includes practical exercises that require the readers to perform the technique and interpret the results, equipping students with the necessary skills to apply statistics by means of SPSS in marketing and consumer research. Finally, there is a list of articles employing the technique that can be used for further reading.

This textbook provides introductory material for advanced undergraduate and postgraduate students studying marketing and consumer analytics, teaching methods along with practical software-applied training using SPSS. Support material includes two real data sets to illustrate the techniques' applications and PowerPoint slides providing a step-by-step guide to the analysis and commented outcomes. Professionals are invited to use the book to select and use the appropriate analytics for their specific context.

José Marcos Carvalho de Mesquita is Professor of Marketing at FUMEC University, Brazil, and visiting researcher at the University of Connecticut, USA.

Erik Kostelijk is Associate Professor of Marketing at the Amsterdam School of International Business of the University of Applied Sciences in Amsterdam, the Netherlands.

Business Analytics

Marketing Analytics
Statistical Tools for Marketing and Consumer Behavior Using SPSS
José Marcos Carvalho de Mesquita and Erik Kostelijk

Marketing Analytics

Statistical Tools for Marketing
and Consumer Behavior Using SPSS

**José Marcos Carvalho de Mesquita
and Erik Kostelijk**

Routledge
Taylor & Francis Group

LONDON AND NEW YORK

First published 2022
by Routledge
2 Park Square, Milton Park, Abingdon, Oxon OX14 4RN

and by Routledge
605 Third Avenue, New York, NY 10158

Routledge is an imprint of the Taylor & Francis Group, an informa business

British Library Cataloguing-in-Publication Data
A catalogue record for this book is available from the British Library

Library of Congress Cataloging-in-Publication Data
Names: Mesquita, José Marcos Carvalho de, author. | Kostelijk, Erik, author.
Title: Marketing analytics : statistical tools for marketing and consumer behaviour using SPSS / José Marcos Carvalho de Mesquita and Erik Kostelijk.
Description: Abingdon, Oxon ; New York, NY : Routledge, 2022. | Series: Business analytics | Includes bibliographical references and index.
Identifiers: LCCN 2021026580
Subjects: LCSH: Marketing—Statistical methods. | Marketing—Data processing. | SPSS (Computer file)
Classification: LCC HF5415.125 .M473 2022 | DDC 658.8/342—dc23
LC record available at https://lccn.loc.gov/2021026580

ISBN: 978-1-032-05218-2 (hbk)
ISBN: 978-1-032-05219-9 (pbk)
ISBN: 978-1-003-19661-7 (ebk)

DOI: 10.4324/9781003196617

Typeset in Times New Roman
by Apex CoVantage, LLC

All Illustrations Reprint Courtesy of International Business Machines Corporation, © International Business Machines Corporation

Access the Support Material: www.routledge.com/9781032052199

Contents

Preface

Over the past decades, marketing theory and marketing practice have been in constant evolution. Marketing gained a central position in most organizations, the importance of corporate social responsibility became a driving force for the emergence of societal marketing, and big data, internet, social media, and influencers have enriched the marketing landscape. New trends emerged and were adopted in the daily business of many organizations.

The importance of marketing accountability in combination with the continuous development in information communications technology has consistently increased the use of marketing analytics and statistical tools supporting both academic and managerial research. As a result, an increasing number of research reports, marketing plans, dissertations, and articles use some statistical methodology. A simple search in conference proceedings and peer-reviewed journals is enough to prove this statement. Similarly, companies increasingly use big data and marketing analytics to evaluate their marketing activities or design new strategies.

With the accelerating use of statistics in academic research and business management, the respective literature must also be improved. Whether teaching classes, participating in committees, evaluating articles, working as a marketing consultant, or even in discussions with fellow researchers or graduate students, we found a lack of didactical material that guides the researcher or the student in the use of quantitative methodology. Likewise, marketing practitioners need some support in conducting market research, especially data analysis.

Although several recent publications have provided useful sources of information, we believe that there is still a lot of ground to be made up. Therefore, we developed this text, which seeks, by using simple language and practical examples, to present a road map for the application of statistical analysis using IBM® SPSS® Statistics Software (SPSS), a software widely used in marketing research.

This book presents the most important analytical techniques in marketing, each chapter devoted to a specific technique. Chapter 1 presents the basic steps to create an SPSS file and to manipulate data. Additionally, we show the basic notions of descriptive statistics. Chapter 2 then introduces exploratory data analysis by providing guidelines for verifying assumptions, or to check the data pattern in terms of normality, homoscedasticity, and linearity. Furthermore, this chapter also addresses the tests to identify outliers and missing data, which are quite common in social sciences data sets.

Chapter 3 introduces analysis of variance (ANOVA) and multivariate analysis of variance (MANOVA), suitable techniques to test the influence of categorical variables, by measuring differences between parameters such as mean and variance. For example, can gender, marital status, or income drive differences in the use of products such as fashionable clothing, foods, and beverage? By using ANOVA/MANOVA, we can uncover consumptions patterns not easily identified in a simple data set.

Chapter 4 presents simple and multiple regression analysis, appropriate techniques to assess the influence of one or more independent metric variables on a dependent metric variable. – for instance, to identify the effect of a price increase on sales. In addition, regression analysis helps analyze the effect of advertising expenditures on sales.

Time series data is a series of observations on values that a variable takes at different points in time, such as hours, days, weeks, months, years, etc. Time series analysis, discussed in Chapter 5, is useful to uncover patterns in the sequence of numbers, such as trends, seasonality, or cycles, or to forecast future patterns. For instance, hotels in touristic cities have high occupation rates in holidays and vacation periods; restaurants, hair dressers, and grocery stores have daily variations, while public transport has hourly patterns. Identifying these patterns can be helpful to manage planning, staffing, or marketing campaigns.

Discriminant analysis, or in some occasions logistic regression, is the appropriate technique to measure the effects of independent metric variables on a categorical dependent variable, divided into two or more groups. This is covered in Chapter 6. For instance, imagine a service provider with high rates of customer defection. Using these techniques, it is possible to identify which variables are causing the customer to remain loyal or to leave.

Then, in Chapter 7, cluster analysis is discussed, a data reduction technique that aims to group cases and not variables; that is, it seeks to identify groups with similar characteristics. It is a useful technique in market segmentation, as we can identify groups of customers with similar behavior and preferences.

In Chapter 8, we discuss Exploratory Factor Analysis (EFA), a technique that seeks to group observable, directly measurable variables in higher order (latent) dimensions. For instance, what is the meaning of service quality? Obviously, it will vary in accordance with the customer profile and the sector. Using EFA, we can identify what dimensions of service quality are most valued by, let's say, fitness centers' customers, such as presence of equipment, opening hours, location, or trainers and staff support.

Chapter 9 presents Confirmatory Factor Analysis (CFA), which aims to confirm if a factor solution is enough robust: instead of looking for dimensions that group observable variables, it seeks to confirm if the relationship between the observable variables and their respective factors are robust. Using CFA, we are able to measure many important variables, such as loyalty, satisfaction, perceived value, switching intention, brand image, etc.

Finally, Chapter 10 discusses Structural Equation Modeling, which deals with the relationships between latent variables. It contains two models: the measurement model, which examines the factor solution, as in CFA, and the structural model, which measures the relationships between the factors (constructs), as in multiple regression. Examples of SEM applications are manifold; we can measure how satisfaction and perceived value influence loyalty or how service quality and complaints handling influence switching intention, among many others.

To illustrate these techniques, we use two data sets. The first relates to a survey on consumer behavior in supermarkets. The questionnaire contains 35 questions about the important attributes when choosing a supermarket store. The sample contains 300 respondents, divided into three income categories: high, medium, and low. The second data set comes from a survey with fitness center customers. It has 25 questions and 300 respondents, all of them customers who faced a service failure and made a complaint. The variables are related to fail severity, justice in handling the complaint, satisfaction with the recovery, and switching intention. After three to four months, there was a follow-up to identify customers who remained and who exited.

Each chapter contains a brief description of the technique, followed by possible marketing applications. One of these examples is then used in detail to illustrate the technique, including the needed SPSS commands and explanation of the SPSS output results. Each chapter ends with a list of exercises that focus on performing the technique, interpreting the results, and designing research in a specific market context. Summing up, each chapter offers support to apply relevant techniques in consumer research. The exercises and applications in the book show how each technique can be applied in a business context, creating a practical feel to the material provided. Finally, there is also a list of articles employing the technique that may be used as a reference guide.

Each chapter contains a rich variety of illustrations to visualize the use of the techniques explained in that chapter. The purpose is to create a hands-on manual that make the use of statistics accessible for every interested student, professional, or researcher. Visually oriented readers are encouraged to use the illustrations in our book, whereas other readers might benefit from the step-by-step descriptions in the text. We would like to point out here that SPSS also offers a wide array of support. For instance, SPSS contains a number of options to stimulate accessibility for visually impaired users; see www.ibm.com/docs/en/stafs/4.0.1?topic=support-accessibility-visually-impaired-users.

All illustrations are reprinted courtesy by International Business Machine Corporation®, SPSS® Statistics software.

The book uses a couple of mathematical formulas to better explain the techniques illustrated in the book. However, we do not use detailed mathematics, as the purpose of the book is the application in marketing practice.

The book also includes support material on the publisher's website. Here you can find the SPSS databases of our two case studies (supermarket and fitness center), and also a set of PowerPoint slides with step-by-step instructions to run the analysis. For this support material, we refer to the e-resources on the publisher's website. The link to these e-resources – at the time of printing this book – is www.routledge.com/9781032052199. Here you can find a link that says "Support Material," and the resources will be available to download there. The link is also provided on the book's cover.

Chapters can be read according to your own interest, with the exception of the first two chapters. Each chapter focuses on a specific technique, and the reader can focus on those techniques that are of his or her specific interest. We hope to contribute to all who would like to take marketing analytics to a higher level and use quantitative methodology and statistics as an essential tool to drive their research or marketing practice. Marketing students are encouraged to use this book as support for doing a market research project or for their thesis.

José Marcos Carvalho de Mesquita
Erik Kostelijk

1 Creating and examining databases in SPSS

IBM SPSS Statistics Software (SPSS) is statistical software widely used in social science studies. SPSS is short for Statistical Package for the Social Sciences. Section 1.1 gives an introduction on how to create an SPSS spreadsheet and how to manipulate data. Section 1.2 illustrates the use of frequency tables, and section 1.3 provides more background on cross tabulations.

In this chapter, as in all the other chapters of this book, you have the opportunity to exercise with the SPSS spreadsheets. For these exercises, we refer to the SPSS files on the e-resources on the publisher's website. The link to these e-resources at the time of printing this book is: www.routledge.com/9781032052199. Here you can find a link that says "Support Material," and the resources will be available to download there. The link is also provided on the book's cover.

1.1 Creating the SPSS spreadsheet and manipulating data

To create a spreadsheet in SPSS, we can input data manually or import from other spreadsheets, such as Excel, or use copy and paste tools. SPSS has only two sheets, Data View and Variable View. Data View contains the data itself, and the Variable View contains the names and variables specifications.

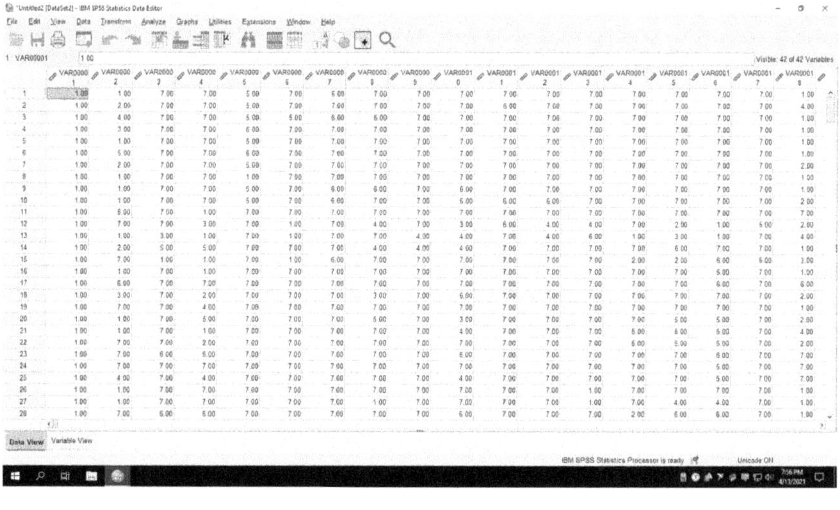

Figure 1.1 Data View sheet.

DOI: 10.4324/9781003196617-1

It is possible to input the variables labels, such as the questions, and the scale values, for example: 1 strongly disagree . . . 7 strongly disagree. There is also information about missing values.

To input the questions, follow the steps:

1   Select "Variable View" sheet;
2   Select the cells;
3   Paste the list of questions.

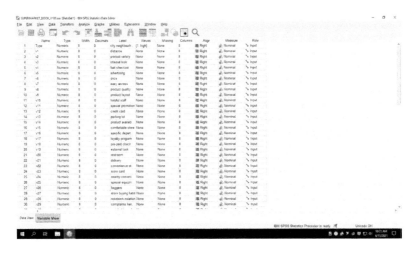

Figure 1.2 Variable View sheet.

To add variables labels, follow the steps:

1   Select "Variable View" sheet;
2   Select and double click the cell in the Value column;
3   Fill in the dialog box, for example, value 1, label male, add;
4   Repeat the steps for the other values;
5   Click "OK."

Figure 1.3 Adding value labels.

If we need to transform any variable, the program allows many options. The following figures show the steps. We use the SPSS file "Supermarket," which you can find in the online material for this book (see publisher's website). For example, to calculate the average (summated scale), do the following:

1 Select "Transform";
2 Select "Compute Variable";
3 Enter name of the target variable (Example: Mean_Product);
4 Choose the function (Example: MEAN);
5 Select variables from which you want to calculate the mean (Example: v2, v8, v9, v14);
6 Click "OK."

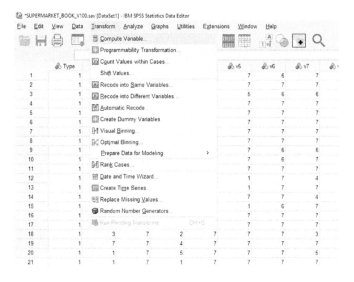

Figure 1.4 Compute variable, I.

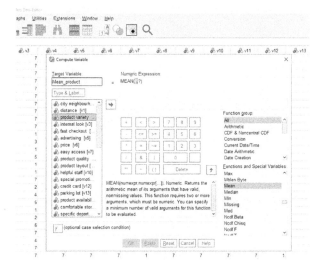

Figure 1.5 Compute variable, II.

To transform an interval scale in a nominal scale (for example, from 1 to 7 into three categories, low, middle, and high):

1 Select "Transform";
2 Select "Recode into different variables";
3 Select input variable (Example: repurchase intention (v35));
4 Choose output variable name (Example: repurchase_group);
5 Click "Change";
6 Click "Old and New Values . . .";
7 Select the values or the range (Example: Range 1 through 2);
8 Create new value (Example: Value: 1);
9 Repeat to include all values. In this example, you will get value 1 (low), value 2 (middle) and value 3 (high);
10 Click "Continue";
11 Click "OK."

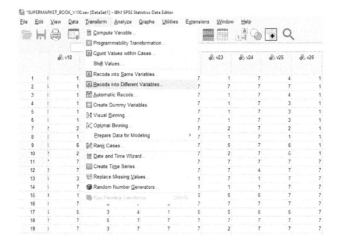

Figure 1.6 Recode into different variable, I.

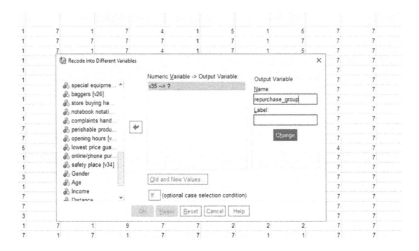

Figure 1.7 Recode into different variable, II.

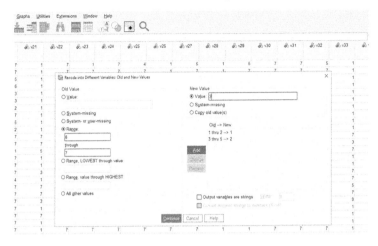

Figure 1.8 Recode into different variable, III.

The newly created values will appear at the end of your SPSS variable and data sheet, like this:

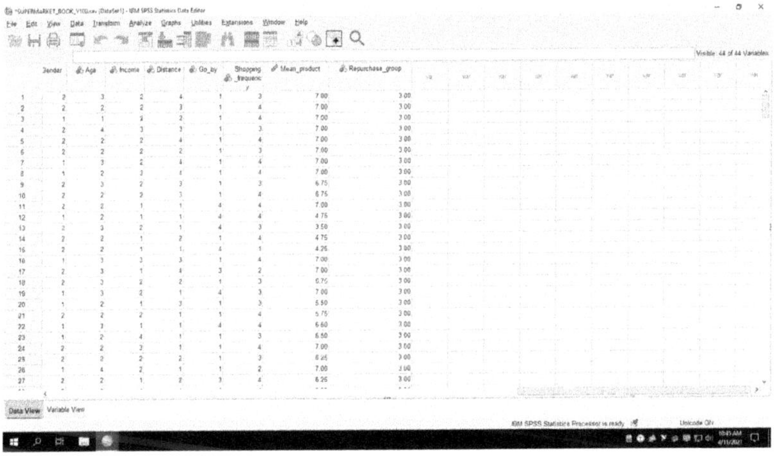

Figure 1.9 Recode into different variable, new variable added.

1.2 Descriptive statistics with frequencies

The frequency of a particular data value is the number of times the data value occurs. For example, if, on a Likert scale ranging from 1 (strongly disagree) to 5 (strongly agree), 12 respondents chose value 1, then the frequency of value 1 is 12. The frequency of a data value is often represented by f.

A frequency table is constructed by arranging collected data values in ascending order of magnitude with their corresponding frequencies.

We will use the supermarket database to illustrate this. Let's consider the importance customers give to the variable price when choosing a store. This variable is measured on a seven-point interval scale, ranging from (1) not at all important to (7) very important. The respondents are split in three groups according to the average income of the neighborhood where they live in, (1) high, (2) middle, and (3) low.

To evaluate the frequency in SPSS, follow the steps:

1 Analyze;
2 Descriptive statistics;
3 Frequencies;
4 Select variable(s);
5 Click OK.

Readers workshop

a Open the supermarket database;
b Perform the analysis, following the steps given above;
c Analyze the frequency;
d Analyze the descriptive statistics.

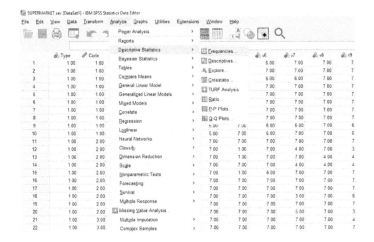

Figure 1.10 Descriptive Statistics – Frequencies, I.

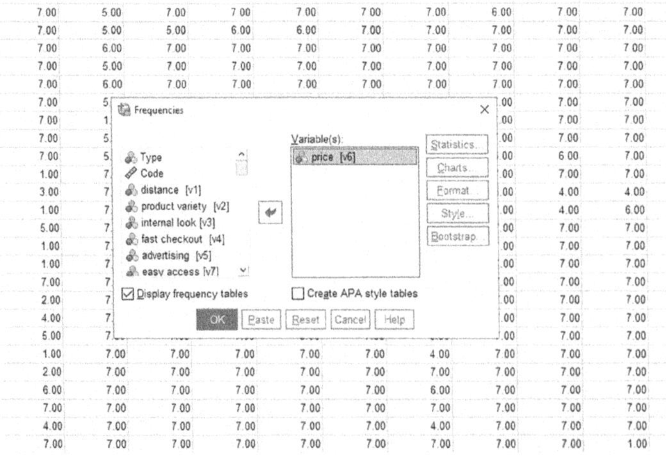

Figure 1.11 Descriptive Statistics – Frequencies, II.

	Frequency	Percent	Valid Percent	Cumulative Percent
Valid 2.00	1	.3	.3	.3
3.00	2	.7	.7	1.0
4.00	13	4.3	4.3	5.3
5.00	43	14.3	14.3	19.7
6.00	91	30.3	30.3	50.0
7.00	150	50.0	50.0	100.0
Total	300	100.0	100.0	

Figure 1.12 Descriptive statistics – frequencies, output.

The outcomes table (Figure 1.12) shows in the first column the options (observe that no respondent chose 1). The frequency of each option appears in the second column, and the corresponding percentage in the third column. The Valid Percent takes the missing data into account. It has the same values as the Percent column if the data set is without missing values. Finally, the cumulative percent shows the sum of the percentages in each row. A frequency table allows a quick review of the data. For example, assuming that 5, 6, and 7 are high evaluation, then price is important for almost 95% of respondents, as the cumulative frequency until 4 is 5.3%.

1.3 Cross tabulation

Cross tabulation (or Crosstab) is a statistical technique that describes two or more variables simultaneously and produces tables that reflect their joint distribution in relation to their related categories or values.

For example, a sales clerk receives both extreme positive and negative evaluations from customers. For example, on a scale from 1 to 7, he or she gets many 1s and many 7s. This disparity is intriguing. Using crosstab, we may observe that the clerk gets the 1s from young people and 7s from the elderly. A deeper analysis could show the reasons. Perhaps the clerk is quite attentive when serving customers; consequently, he or she works slowly, which makes young customers angry and older customers happy.

To illustrate how to run a crosstab, we use the database Gym, which contains variables concerning service failure, complaint handling, switching intention, and actual exit. Actual exit refers to churn, the customers that end their subscription to the gym. We want to figure out if churn (measured by the variable named follow up: 1 = remain; 2 = exit) is associated with any specific type of fail, grouped in three categories: (1) equipment, (2) personnel, and (3) infrastructure.

To run the analysis, the steps are:

1 Analyze;
2 Descriptive Statistics;
3 Crosstabs;
4 Select row variable (fail_group);
5 Select column variable (follow-up);
6 Statistics (check Chi-Square and contingency coefficient);
7 Cells: counts: check observed; percentage: check column;
8 OK.

Readers workshop

a   Open the gym database;
b   Perform the analysis, following the steps listed;
c   Analyze the frequency;
d   Analyze the Chi-Square test.

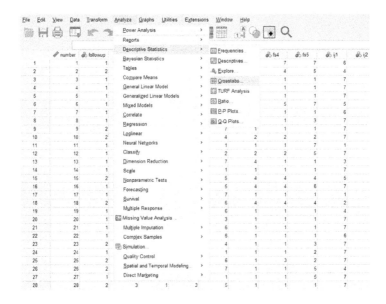

Figure 1.13 Crosstabs, I.

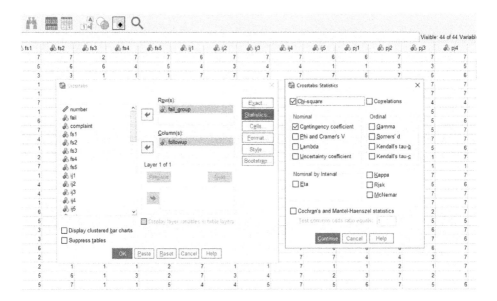

Figure 1.14 Crosstabs, II.

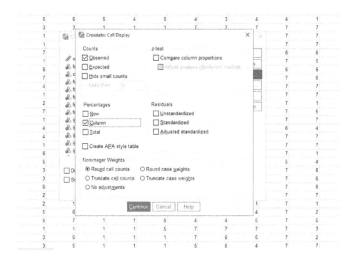

Figure 1.15 Crosstabs, III.

Out of 300 reported fails, as showed in column total, 125 were from group 1, 99 from group 2, and 76 from group 3. Turning to column 2, we see that 119 customers stopped their membership at the fitness center. Out of these leaving customers, 55 (46.2%) did this because of personnel fails. Thus, although failures of the fitness center personnel accounts for a smaller number of occurrences (33%), they cause more damage in customer retention. The (Pearson) Chi-Square test (15.874) shows a significant difference if asymptotic significance < 0.050, as is the case here.

| | | | Follow-up | | |
			Permanence	Defection	Total
fail_group	equipment	Count	87	38	125
		% within follow-up	48.1%	31.9%	41.7%
	personnel	Count	44	55	99
		% within follow-up	24.3%	46.2%	33.0%
	infrastructure	Count	50	26	76
		% within follow-up	27.6%	21.8%	25.3%
Total		Count	181	119	300
		% within follow-up	100.0%	100.0%	100.0%

Figure 1.16 Crosstabs output, I.

	Value	df	Asymptotic Significance (2-sided)
Pearson Chi-Square	15.874[a]	2	.000
Likelihood Ratio	15.762	2	.000
Linear-by-Linear Association	1.193	1	.275
N of Valid Cases	300		

a. 0 cells (0.0%) have expected count less than 5. The minimum expected count is 30.15.

Figure 1.17 Crosstabs output, II.

If we want to refine the analysis, we can include a third variable, such as gender (1 = male; 2 = female). We must follow the same steps, and add the variable gender at "layer." We observe that men reported more equipment fail (47.5%), but the defection rate is smaller (38.5%). However, 40.1% of women complaints were due to personnel but caused 56.3% of defections. The differences are significant only for the women.

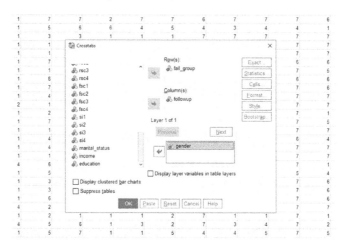

Figure 1.18 Crosstabs, IV.

| Gender | | | | | Follow-up | | |
					Permanence	Defection	Total
male	fail_group	equipment	Count		41	15	56
			% within follow-up		51.9%	38.5%	47.5%
		personnel	Count		16	10	26
			% within follow-up		20.3%	25.6%	22.0%
		infrastructure	Count		22	14	36
			% within follow-up		27.8%	35.9%	30.5%
	Total		Count		79	39	118
			% within follow-up		100.0%	100.0%	100.0%
female	fail_group	equipment	Count		46	23	69
			% within follow-up		45.1%	28.7%	37.9%
		personnel	Count		28	45	73
			% within follow-up		27.5%	56.3%	40.1%
		infrastructure	Count		28	12	40
			% within follow-up		27.5%	15.0%	22.0%
	Total		Count		102	80	182
			% within follow-up		100.0%	100.0%	100.0%

Figure 1.19 Crosstabs output, III.

Gender				Follow-up Permanence	Defection	Total
Total	fail_group	equipment	Count	87	38	125
			% within follow-up	48.1%	31.9%	41.7%
		personnel	Count	44	55	99
			% within follow-up	24.3%	46.2%	33.0%
		infrastructure	Count	50	26	76
			% within follow-up	27.6%	21.8%	25.3%
	Total		Count	181	119	300
			% within follow-up	100.0%	100.0%	100.0%

Figure 1.19 (Continued)

Gender		Value	df	Asymptotic Significance (2-sided)
male	Pearson Chi-Square	1.892[b]	2	.388
	Likelihood Ratio	1.906	2	.386
	Linear-by-Linear Association	1.592	1	.207
	N of Valid Cases	118		
female	Pearson Chi-Square	15.594[c]	2	.000
	Likelihood Ratio	15.728	2	.000
	Linear-by-Linear Association	.118	1	.731
	N of Valid Cases	182		
Total	Pearson Chi-Square	15.874[a]	2	.000
	Likelihood Ratio	15.762	2	.000
	Linear-by-Linear Association	1.193	1	.275
	N of Valid Cases	300		

a. 0 cells (0.0%) have expected count less than 5. The minimum expected count is 30.15.
b. 0 cells (0.0%) have expected count less than 5. The minimum expected count is 8.59.
c. 0 cells (0.0%) have expected count less than 5. The minimum expected count is 17.58.

Figure 1.20 Crosstabs output, IV

2 Introduction to exploratory data analysis

Exploratory data analysis must precede any application of multivariate statistical techniques. This is an important step to identify patterns in the data, especially the existence of outliers and missing data, and the assumptions' verification, among which we highlight data linearity, normality, and homoscedasticity.

Section 2.1 introduces exploratory data analysis and its application in IBM SPSS Statistics Software (SPSS). Section 2.2. is dedicated to the verification of the assumptions of normality, homoscedasticity, and linearity. Section 2.3 discusses the identification of possible outliers, and section 2.4 is devoted to missing values. As in most of the other chapters, this chapter ends with some exercise material, an exercise in which the student can practice with the techniques of this chapter, and a market insight that applies the theory to a professional context.

2.1 Exploratory data analysis

Descriptive statistics are very useful in allowing a comprehensive view of the data set, as they provide information that describe how the data is distributed. Information obtained by calculating central tendency and dispersion measures is often the first step in exploratory data analysis. The following describes the meanings of a number of these measures.

Central tendency measures

Central tendency measures are used to indicate a value that tends to typify, or better represent, a set of numbers. That is, a set of data in its raw form does not provide much information, but when this data set is represented by a central tendency measure, it takes on a much more explicit meaning. The most common central tendency measures are: (arithmetic) mean, median, and mode.

Arithmetic mean: $$\bar{x} = \frac{\sum_{i=1}^{n} x_i}{n}$$

The mean represents the sum of all elements divided by the number of elements. In general, it is the most used measure, but it has the deficiency of being very affected by extreme values: if some values are a lot higher or lower than the others, this tends to raise or substantially reduce the average values.

Median: divides a set of data into two equal groups. It can be calculated following these steps:

1   Sort the values, ascending or descending;
2   Check if the number of elements is even or odd;

DOI: 10.4324/9781003196617-2

3   If it is odd, the median is the middle value;
4   If it is even, the median is the arithmetic mean of the two central values.

Mode: value that occurs most frequently. For its identification, simple counting is enough.

Dispersion measures

Dispersion measures indicate how far the data are from the average value, that is, they show the dispersion of the elements in relation to the data central point. There are several dispersion measures, and statistical software provides many of them, but the most used are variance and standard deviation. The interpretation of both measures is relatively simple: a low variance (or standard deviation) means that most data are close to the mean, whereas a higher variance (or standard deviation) implies a higher spread of data in relation to the mean. Here, we discuss in more detail range, variance, and standard deviation.

   Range: difference between the highest and the lowest values (maximum − minimum).

Variance: $\sigma_x^2 = \dfrac{\Sigma\left(X_i - \bar{X}\right)^2}{n-1}$

The variance is the sum of the squared deviation of each observation (X_i) in relation to the mean value $(\bar{X})$, divided by the number of elements (n). Because the population variance is supposed to have a bigger value, we use $(n - 1)$ as the denominator when estimating from a sample data. The variance has a serious limitation, as it shows the dispersion in a squared measurement unit. For this reason, one can use the standard deviation, which is exactly the square root of the variance.

Standard Deviation: $\sigma_x^2 = \sqrt[2]{\dfrac{\Sigma\left(X_i - \bar{X}\right)^2}{n-1}}$

A simple analysis of the formulas shows how difficult it would be to calculate any of the measures described earlier, which becomes even more so when the number of elements in the data set grows. The use of spreadsheets simplifies the task, and the statistical packages provide results instantly.

   There are many options to perform an exploratory data analysis in SPSS. We use the following set of steps, that include most tests needed for this chapter:

1   Analyze;
2   Descriptive Statistics;
3   Explore;
4   Select the variable(s) in the dialog (dependent list);
5   Select the grouping variable (factor list), if necessary;
6   Statistics: select Descriptives and Outliers;
7   Plots:

    a   Boxplot: select Factor levels together;
    b   Descriptive: select Stem-and-leaf, Histogram;

  c Select Normality plots with tests;
  d Spread vs Level with Levene Test: select Power Estimation;

8 Continue;
9 OK.

We use the supermarket database to illustrate this analysis. Let's consider the importance customers give to the variable price (v6) when choosing a store, measured in a seven-point interval scale, ranging from (1) not at all important to (7) very important. We want to check if the importance of price depends on the type of neighborhood where they live. The respondents were split in three types of neighborhood (Type, the first variable in the SPSS spreadsheet): 1 (neighborhood with on average high income), 2 (middle income), and 3 (low income).

 For the example, please use the following steps as guidelines:

Readers workshop

a Open the supermarket database;
b Perform the analysis, following the steps in the previous section;
c Check the existence of missing data;
d Check the data normality, homoscedasticity, and linearity;
e Check the existence of univariate outliers;
f Check the existence of outliers;

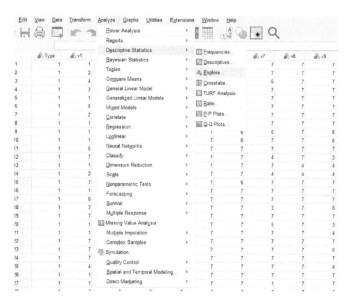

Figure 2.1 Exploratory data analysis, I.

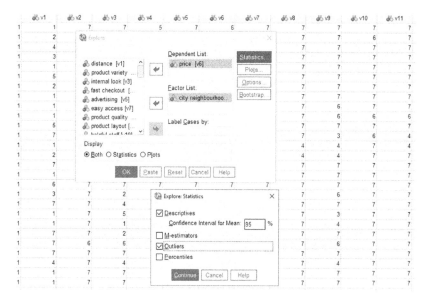

Figure 2.2 Exploratory data analysis, II.

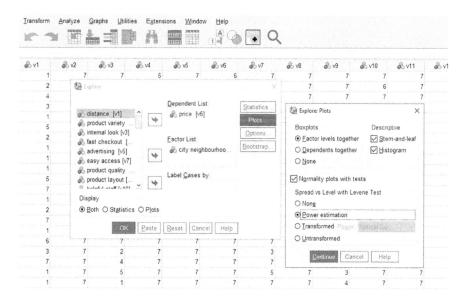

Figure 2.3 Exploratory data analysis, III.

The first output table gives a brief description of the data: variable (price), the groups (city region income), number of cases in each group (*N*), and the missing cases.

City Region Income		Cases					
		Valid		Missing		Total	
		N	Percent	*N*	Percent	*N*	Percent
price	high	100	100.0%	0	0.0%	100	100.0%
	middle	100	100.0%	0	0.0%	100	100.0%
	low	100	100.0%	0	0.0%	100	100.0%

Figure 2.4 Exploratory data analysis, Output, I.

Type				Statistic	Std. Error
price	high	Mean		6.2800	.08771
		95% Confidence Interval for Mean	Lower Bound	6.1060	
			Upper Bound	6.4540	
		5% Trimmed Mean		6.3556	
		Median		7.0000	
		Variance		.937	
		Std. Deviation		.87709	
		Minimum		4.00	
		Maximum		7.00	
		Range		3.00	
		Interquartile Range		1.00	
		Skewness		−.950	.241
		Kurtosis		−.097	.478
	middle	Mean		6.1600	.09611
		95% Confidence Interval for Mean	Lower Bound	5.9693	
			Upper Bound	6.3507	
		5% Trimmed Mean		6.2444	
		Median		6.0000	
		Variance		.924	
		Std. Deviation		.96106	
		Minimum		3.00	
		Maximum		7.00	
		Range		4.00	
		Interquartile Range		1.00	
		Skewness		−1.095	.241
		Kurtosis		.634	.478
	low	Mean		6.2700	.09729
		95% Confidence Interval for Mean	Lower Bound	6.0770	
			Upper Bound	6.4630	
		5% Trimmed Mean		6.3778	
		Median		7.0000	
		Variance		.947	
		Std. Deviation		.97292	
		Minimum		2.00	
		Maximum		7.00	
		Range		5.00	
		Interquartile Range		1.00	
		Skewness		−1.644	.241
		Kurtosis		3.544	.478

Figure 2.5 Exploratory data analysis, output, II.

The second table in the output is the "Descriptives" table. Customers attribute to price the following mean importance – 6.28, 6.16, and 6.27 – and the standard deviations are .877, .961, and .973, for high-, middle-, and low-income neighborhood, respectively. Apparently, price is considered very important, irrespective of customers' income. The medians are 7, 6, and 7 and the variances .937, .924, and .947, respectively. The output shows also the 95% confidence interval for means; the minimum and the maximum values; the range; and the interquartile range. The mode is not provided, and its estimation would involve the same sequence to estimate the frequency. In the results table (Figure 1.12 in the previous chapter), check the option with the highest number of responses. We can see that option 7, with 150 responses, is the mode.

For the skewness and kurtosis in the "Descriptives" table, we refer to the next section.

2.2 Verification of assumptions

Verifying assumptions corresponds to a fundamental step in many multivariate techniques, but its importance varies from technique to technique. Initially, we must perform an analysis to verify the occurrence of three assumptions:

- Normality;
- Homoscedasticity;
- Linearity.

Normality

The normal distribution is one of the most used probability distributions in different research areas. It indicates the data distribution around the mean and shows that 90% of the elements are between +1 and −1 standard deviation from the mean, 95% are between +2 and −2, and 99% between +3 and −3. In the normal distribution, mean, mode, and median present the same values.

Several significance tests start from the assumption that the distribution is normal, including the F and χ^2 tests, which implies the need for verification. The required normality refers to multivariate normality, which is very specific and not provided by most statistical packages. Therefore, we limit ourselves here to a discussion of univariate normality. We address some attention to multivariate normality in Chapters 9 and 10.

To assess univariate normality, SPSS provides some specific statistics, in addition to measures of kurtosis and asymmetry.

	Type	Kolmogorov–Smirnov[a]			Shapiro–Wilk		
		Statistic	df	Sig.	Statistic	df	Sig.
price	high	.314	100	.000	.768	100	.000
	middle	.259	100	.000	.793	100	.000
	low	.303	100	.000	.738	100	.000

a. Lilliefors Significance Correction

Figure 2.6 Test of normality.

Two normality tests are presented: Kolmogorov–Smirnov and Shapiro–Wilks. For both, test statistics (.314 and .768; .259 and .793; .303 and .738, for high, middle, and low, respectively), degrees of freedom (100 and 100) and significance levels (.000 and .000) are provided (Figure 2.6).

The hypothesis (H_0) supposes data normality. With a significance level (Sig.) < 0.050, H_0 is rejected, implying that the data distribution is not normal. The significance level .000 indicates the H_0 rejection, confirming that the data do not have a normal distribution.

This finding is reinforced by the histogram (Figure 2.7), which indicates the class interval on the horizontal axis and the observations' relative frequency on the vertical axis. For instance, in the low-income neighborhood, it appears that the frequency distribution is more concentrated on the right, that is, there are more observations above the average.

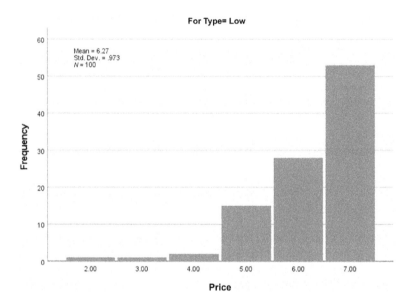

Figure 2.7 Test of normality, histogram.

The stem-and-leaf graphic confirms this conclusion. It shows in the first column the relative frequency of each possible response and in the second (stem) the possible responses themselves; in the third column (leaves), each 0 indicates an answer. For the sake of simplicity, only the output for the low-income category is presented (the same output as was visualized in the histogram). There are 4 responses below or equal to grade 4, 15 equal 5, 28 equal 6, and 53 respondents marked grade 7.

In addition to these measures, kurtosis and asymmetry statistics also assess the distribution normality. In the case of the normal distribution, mean, mode, and median assume the same value.

The skewness shows the data concentration in certain values, whether in the center, to the right, or to the left of the mean. The value for a symmetric distribution is 0, a negative value indicates concentration on the right, and positive indicates concentration on the left. When the asymmetry is greater than +1 or smaller than −1, the distribution is substantially asymmetric.

Kurtosis shows whether the data are very concentrated around the mean (peak) or very distributed (flat). There is no cutoff point, but positive values indicate peak distribution and negative values indicate flat distribution.

```
price Stem-and-Leaf Plot for
Type= low

 Frequency     Stem &  Leaf

     4.00 Extremes      (=<4.0)
    15.00           5 .  000000000000000
     .00            5 .
     .00            5 .
     .00            5 .
     .00            5 .
    28.00           6 .  0000000000000000000000000000
     .00            6 .
     .00            6 .
     .00            6 .
     .00            6 .
    53.00           7 .  00000000000000000000000000000000000000000000000000000
 Stem width:       1.00
 Each leaf:          1 case(s)
```

Figure 2.8 Test of normality, stem-and-leaf.

By the results presented in the "Descriptives" table, for low income, the skewness value is −1.644, revealing data concentrated to the right of the mean. The kurtosis statistic, in turn, is +3.544, exposing a peak distribution, which was already showed by the histogram and stem-and-leaf graph.

Homoscedasticity

Homoscedasticity primarily refers to the assumption that two sets of data have equivalent variances. It means that the error term is about the same for all values of the data, that is, the error terms do not increase or decrease along the series. In the case of a single variable, homoscedasticity can be verified, as long as there are different groups or measurement categories. The tested null hypothesis would be the following:

$$H_0 = \sigma_1^2 = \sigma_2^2 = \sigma_n^2$$

against the H_1, where at least one variance differs from the others.

In our example, the importance of price when choosing a retail outlet was assessed by consumers from three different income categories, so it can be tested whether the variances in each subset are equivalent.

In SPSS, the syntax of some multivariate techniques already includes this test, but in the exploratory analysis, the script should include "*spread vs. Level with Levene Test, power estimation.*"

The table below shows the results. There are four different tests, each one based in a central tendency measure. The Levene statistic is not significant; consequently, we do not reject H_0. This implies that we can confirm that the variances are equivalent. Thus, there is homoscedasticity: the error term is equivalent along the data series.

		Levene Statistic	df1	df2	Sig.
price	Based on Mean	.056	2	297	.946
	Based on Median	.014	2	297	.986
	Based on Median and with Adjusted *df*	.014	2	268.519	.986
	Based on Trimmed Mean	.045	2	297	.956

Figure 2.9 Test of homoscedasticity.

Linearity

Linearity means that the relationship between two variables is linear, that is, it can be described by a first-degree function. Many multivariate techniques are based on correlational measures, with linearity being a basic assumption. If the data do not show linearity, this assumption is violated, often implying that significant statistical relationships are not identified.

To identify linearity, there are two alternatives:

* Build dispersion diagrams, or
* Calculate the correlation matrix.

Let's measure the relation between opening hours and repurchase intention. We start with building the dispersion diagram. The steps are:

1 Graphs;
2 Legacy Dialogs;
3 Scatter/Dot;
4 Simple Scatter;
5 Define variables in the dialog box (Y axis, X axis);
6 OK

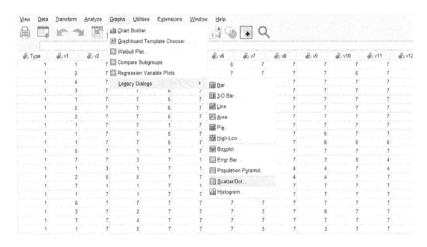

Figure 2.10 Test of linearity, dispersion diagram, I.

Figure 2.11 Test of linearity, dispersion diagram, II.

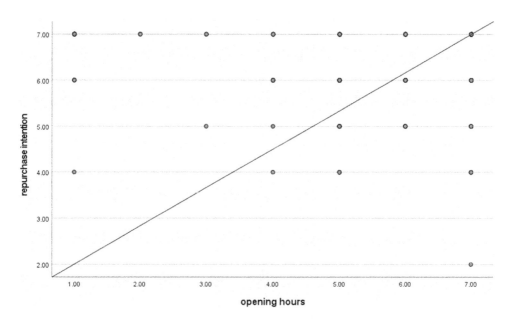

Figure 2.12 Test of linearity, dispersion diagram, output

The alternative is to calculate the correlation coefficient. This can be done with the following procedure:

1 Analyze;
2 Correlate;

3   Bivariate;
4   Check "Pearson" and select variables in the dialog box;
5   Click "OK."

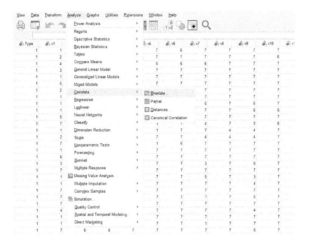

Figure 2.13 Test of linearity, correlation matrix, I.

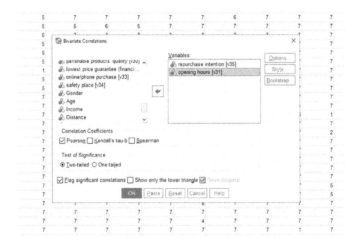

Figure 2.14 Test of linearity, correlation matrix, II.

		Repurchase Intention	Opening Hours
repurchase intention	Pearson Correlation	1	−.020
	Sig. (2-tailed)		.729
	N	300	300
opening hours	Pearson Correlation	−.020	1
	Sig. (2-tailed)	.729	
	N	300	300

Figure 2.15 Test of linearity, correlation matrix, output.

Both the graphical analysis and the correlation coefficient (−0.020, not significant) indicate a nonlinear relationship between the variables. The trendline displayed in the graphic shows clearly the absence of correlation; the cases do not follow the tendency. As an example, some points show customers who graded opening hours as 1 and repurchase intention as 7, but there are also customers who graded the opposite: opening hours as 7 and repurchase intention as 2.

2.3 Outliers

Also called extreme values, they are those that present very different values in relation to the other values included in the data set. They can be the result of errors in data entry, typing, or questionnaire marking, but they can also represent a real value of the set, which tends to distort the mean.

At first, its inclusion or exclusion from the database cannot be assessed simply by the statistical effect, but it depends on a qualitative analysis of how representative that case is. For example, a liquor store is forecasting the cash flow for the next year. If during 11 months the store sold an average of 1,000 units/month of a certain beer, but in a specific month it sold 10,000 due to the occurrence of a music festival in the city, the monthly average increases to 1,750. Should this extreme value remain or be deleted from the database? The answer must take into account the research purposes. If it is to guide monthly orders, it should be deleted; if it is to make the annual budget, it should remain, as long as the festival is scheduled to take place again.

The identification of univariate outliers in SPSS can be done using boxplot graphics, by checking outliers in the script used for exploratory analysis.

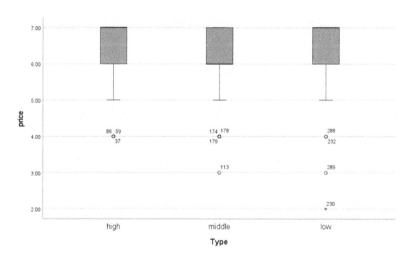

Figure 2.16 Outliers, boxplot.

The box graph presents a box that contains the two internal quartiles of the distribution (50% of the values). Outliers, marked as stars, are those cases 2.5 standard deviation away from the box edge. In our example, there is only one in the low group (230). The other cases, although out of the box, are not considered outliers, as they do not stand 2.5 standard deviations from the edges.

2.4 Missing values

It is quite common in social science research to have missing data. This can be caused by many reasons. It may be due to problems in the data entry process, mistakes in filling the questionnaire, questions not being applicable, or respondents refusing to answer, etc. Some missing data have random causes. In many cases, however, they could be associated with other variables. For example, a certain group of respondents may refuse to inform about their income or marital status; some customers might not be able to evaluate a variable, the store parking lot, for example, because they don't use it.

Thus, the presence of missing data is acceptable and predictable; however, it is important to assess what the cause is and to what extent the data will affect the results, and the remedies that can be taken, as well. As our Supermarket data set does not have any missing data, we will use a hypothetical file for illustration purposes.

To identify the number of missing data, simply run the frequency analysis:

1   Analyze;
2   Descriptives;
3   Frequencies;
4   Select variables.

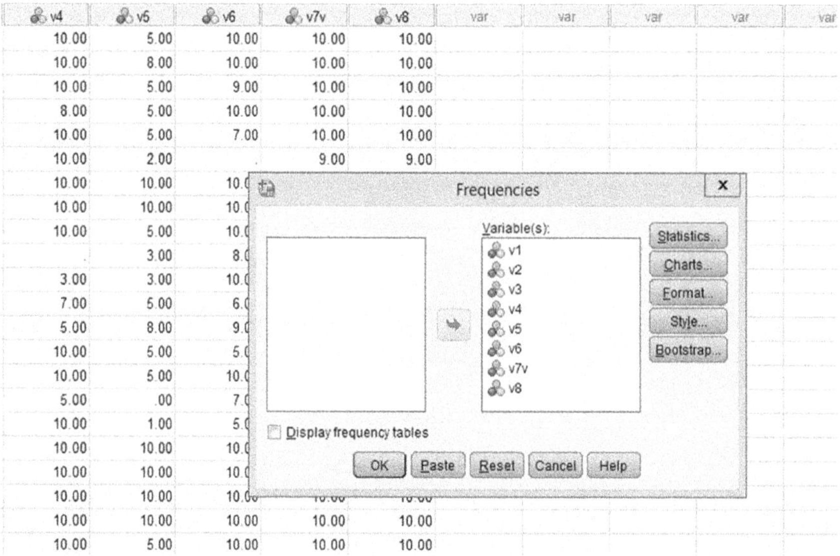

Figure 2.17 Missing values, I.

		v1	v2	v3	v4	v5	v6	v7v	v8
N	Valid	146	149	136	149	148	149	148	148
	Missing	5	2	15	2	3	2	3	3

Figure 2.18 Missing values, output.

Exercise

A manufacturer of high-end fashion, concerned about the growth in the sale of counterfeit goods, conducted a survey to assess the relationship between gender, income, and purchase of these products. The purchase behavior was measured using a seven-points interval scale, ranging from (1) never to (7) frequently. The tables below present the descriptive results concerning gender.

1 Which group presents the highest purchase behavior?
2 Which is most homogenous?
3 Are the data normally distributed?
4 Are the variances equivalent?
5 Are there any outliers?

Gender				Statistic	Std. Error
Purchase Male	Mean			3.5985	.15051
	95% Confidence Interval for Mean	Lower Bound		3.3007	
		Upper Bound		3.8962	
	5% Trimmed Mean			3.5539	
	Median			4.0000	
	Variance			2.990	
	Std. Deviation			1.72923	
	Minimum			1.00	
	Maximum			7.00	
	Range			6.00	
	Interquartile Range			3.00	
	Skewness			.137	.211
	Kurtosis			−.917	.419
Female	Mean			3.7684	.12172
	95% Confidence Interval for Mean	Lower Bound		3.5282	
		Upper Bound		4.0086	
	5% Trimmed Mean			3.7605	
	Median			4.0000	
	Variance			2.622	
	Std. Deviation			1.61931	
	Minimum			1.00	
	Maximum			7.00	
	Range			6.00	
	Interquartile Range			2.00	
	Skewness			−.065	.183
	Kurtosis			−.773	.363

Figure 2.19 Exercise, I.

	Gender	Kolmogorov–Smirnov[a]			Shapiro–Wilk		
		Statistic	df	Sig.	Statistic	df	Sig.
Purchase	Male	.141	132	.000	.938	132	.000
	Female	.139	177	.000	.945	177	.000

a. Lilliefors significance correction.

Figure 2.20 Exercise, II.

		Levene Statistic	df1	df2	Sig.
Purchase	Based on Mean	1.783	1	307	.183
	Based on Median	1.749	1	307	.187
	Based on Median and with Adjusted *df*	1.749	1	306.816	.187
	Based on Trimmed Mean	1.830	1	307	.177

Figure 2.21 Exercise, III.

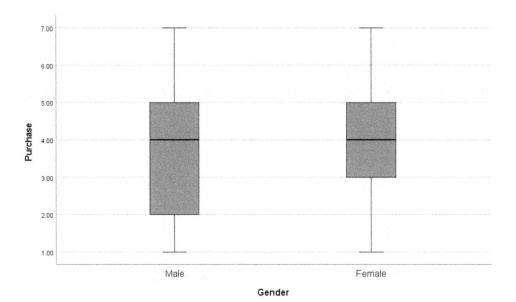

Figure 2.22 Exercise, IV.

Market insight

Enterprise Resource Planning (ERP) is a system that integrates business processes. Among the information that an ERP system provides, the record of sales per period has a great importance in supply chain management.

Considering this information, how can information such as average sales and standard deviation be used to help supply chain management? How can the correlation coefficient help sales increase?

3 Analysis of variance

In many situations, the researcher is faced with the need to test whether there are statistically significant differences between two or more parameters, for example, to test whether the means are equal or to test the equivalence between the variances of many data sets.

To test the differences between two parameters, the "*t*-test" can be used, which will indicate, with a predetermined level of significance, whether the means are different or not. This is explained in section 3.1.

However, in many cases, it may be necessary to test the difference between more than two parameters simultaneously, which makes the use of the *t*-test unfeasible. In these cases, *t*-tests can be performed to test parameters two by two, but for comparing more than two parameters simultaneously, the appropriate technique is ANOVA (for univariate analysis of variance) or MANOVA (for multivariate analysis of variance). ANOVA is explained in sections 3.2, 3.3, and 3.4, MANOVA in sections 3.5 and 3.6.

3.1 Application of *t*-test in SPSS

For this application we use the supermarket database. Let's check if the availability of a parking lot is evaluated in a different way by men and women,

The *t*-test in IBM SPSS Statistics Software (SPSS) requires the following steps:

1 Analyze;
2 Compare Means;
3 Independent Samples T test;
4 Select test variable (v13 = parking lot);
5 Select grouping variable (gender), and define groups (1 and 2);
6 Options: leave the default, then Continue;
7 OK.

First, the program shows the descriptive (Group Statistics). Men (group 1) gave higher rates than women (group 2) for parking lots. The table Independent Samples Test (Figure 3.5) presents the results. We first need to check the equality of variances. The Levene's test is significant (Sig. < 0.05) This implies that variances in the two groups (men and women) are not equal. Then we must consider the second row. As the significance level is .000, men and women attribute different importance to the presence of a parking lot.

DOI: 10.4324/9781003196617-3

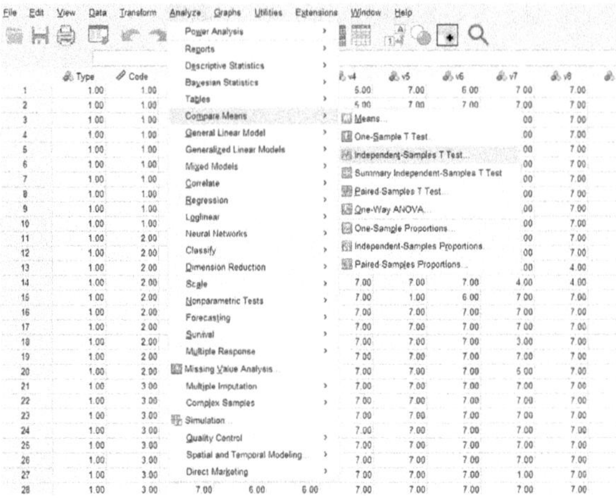

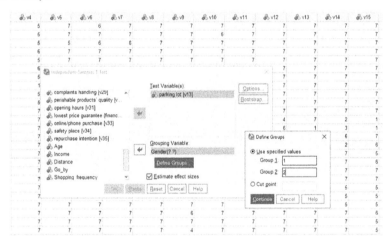

Figure 3.1 T-test, I.

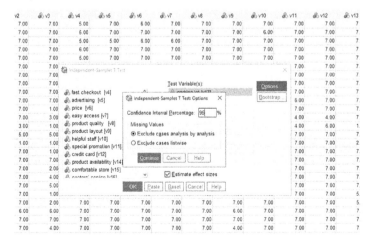

Figure 3.2 T-test, II.

Figure 3.3 T-test, III.

	Gender	N	Mean	Std. Deviation	Std. Error Mean
parking lot	1.00	111	4.8018	2.49297	.23662
	2.00	189	3.7249	2.62323	.19081

Figure 3.4 T-test, output, I.

		Levene's Test for Equality of Variances		T-test for Equality of Means						
									95% Confidence Interval of the Difference	
		F	Sig.	t	df	Sig. (2-tailed)	Mean Difference	Std. Error Difference	Lower	Upper
parking lot	Equal variances assumed	3.916	.049	3.496	298	.001	1.0769	.3080	.4707	1.683
	Equal variances not assumed			3.543	240.15	.000	1.0769	.3039	.4781	1.675

Figure 3.5 T-test, output, II.

3.2 Theoretical background – analysis of variance (ANOVA)

ANOVA is used when the objective is to test the influence of categorical independent variables on a metric dependent variable, such that:

$$Y_1 = X_1 + X_2 + X_3 + \ldots + X_n$$

Wherein:
Y_1 is the metric dependent variable;
X_1, X_2, X_3, up to X_n are the categorical independent variables.

   An independent variable, also called a factor, is usually analyzed in several categories, with each specific category being called a treatment. As an illustration, imagine a survey whose objective is to assess whether there are differences between the store loyalty – a metric dependent variable – of customers with different income – a categorical independent variable, with three treatments, low, middle, and high. Another example would be to test the difference between the use of fashion clothes by people of different marital status, single, married, divorced, or widowed.
   The analysis of variance tests, in short, if the data dispersion within the group is proportionally large in relation to the variance between the groups. Graphically, we have the following situation:

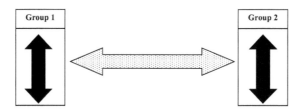

Figure 3.6 ANOVA: Variance within group versus variance between groups.

If the variance within groups (the black arrows) is not different from the variation between groups, the dotted arrow, the categorization does not have any effect on the dependent variable. If the variation within groups is relatively small in relation to the variation between groups (as in the figure), the categorization causes effects on the dependent variable. In this situation, for instance, income would influence loyalty or marital status would influence fashion clothes usage.

The estimation procedure can be done according to the steps described here.

Compute the variance within groups: $SS_{within} = \sum_{c}^{j}\sum_{i}^{n}(Y_{ij} - \bar{Y})^2$

Compute variance between groups: $SS_{between} = \sum_{j=1}^{c} n(\bar{Y}_j - \bar{Y})^2$

Compute F statistic: $F = \dfrac{SS_{between}\big/(c-1)}{SS_{within}\big/(n-c)}$

The ratio between the mean squares represents the variance that can be attributed to the different treatments (within) in relation to the variance attributable to the randomness of the sample (between). If the F statistic is large enough, the treatments actually have an effect on the dependent variable.

3.3 Marketing application of ANOVA

Analysis of variance is useful in many marketing situations. Here we list a couple of examples.

- Marketing experiments testing consumers' responses to different types of treatment. For example, in a taste test, three groups of customers receive a cup of chocolate milk, in which the quantity of chocolate is different for each group. After tasting, participants rate the taste on an interval scale. The differences in ratings can be compared by using ANOVA.
- To test what type of website will be more effective in increasing the sales of a new product, an experiment could submit prospects to two or more website designs, with variations in use of color, text, or illustrations, and test if there are differences in how they are able to trigger consumers' desire to test and purchase the product.
- An experiment in the form of an A/B-test that aims to test which type of ad or website is most effective in triggering consumers' desire or their intention to purchase a product or service.
- The prices of three groups of products (e.g., cheese, laundry detergent, and shower gel) are collected in retail stores located in different neighborhoods, let's say, upper-class, middle-class, and lower-class neighborhoods. Then, it is possible to measure if the pricing of the product groups is different in the three neighborhoods. This test serves the purpose of evaluating whether the store location influences the price policy.
- Sometimes, purchase preferences are influenced by demographic variables. Identifying these preferences is helpful in market segmentation. Consumers with different profiles in terms of marital status, age, or gender are asked to evaluate their attitude towards fashion clothes and average expenses. Will some group have a more favorable attitude or spend more?
- Sales of some products have a seasonal pattern, such as chocolate during Easter, or flowers on Valentine's day. Although the seasonality is certain, the sales volume is

unpredictable. By using ANOVA, a manager can measure if losses and profitability of seasonal products are different, bigger or smaller, than regular ones.

- Loyalty and its two dimensions, repurchase and attitude, are commonly measured in relation to the product, service, or provider features. However, sociodemographic variables may have an effect on loyalty. Which groups are more loyal, male or female, single or married, teenagers or adults?

3.4 Application of ANOVA in SPSS

ANOVA in SPSS requires the following steps:

1 Analyze;
2 Compare Means;
3 One-Way ANOVA;
4 Select variable(s) for the Dependent List (in our example, we use v35 repurchase intention);
5 Select variable as Factor (independent variable) (in this example: type – the average income in the neighborhood, with 3 levels: low (1), middle (2), and high (3));
6 Options: choose Descriptive and Homogeneity test of variance, then Continue;
7 Post Hoc: then select any, for instance Tukey, then Continue;
8 OK.

Readers workshop

a Open the supermarket database;
b Test if income impacts repurchase intention, by following the steps listed;
c Analyze the descriptive;
d Check the data homoscedasticity;
e Test if income has effect on repurchase intention;
f Test which income levels have effect on repurchase intention;
g Test if gender moderates the effects of income on repurchase intention.

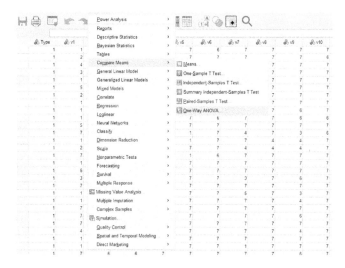

Figure 3.7 ANOVA, I.

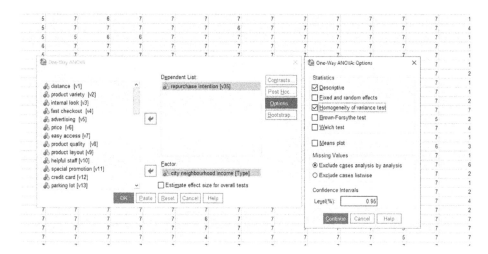

Figure 3.8 ANOVA, II.

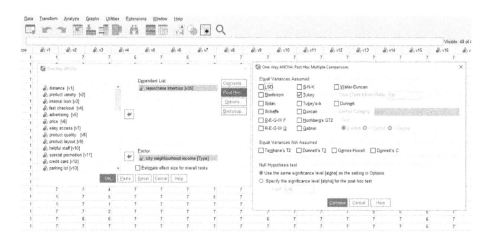

Figure 3.9 ANOVA, III.

First, the outcome will show the descriptive. Figure 3.10 shows the basic statistics described in Chapter 1. Apparently, both the means and the standard deviations are quite similar for each of the three income levels. Figure 3.11 shows the test of homogeneity of variances, one assumption in ANOVA. By the results, we can assume the variances are not equivalent. As the samples are the same size and also because of the number of observations, we can disregard this violation. Next comes the ANOVA table (Figure 3.12). The F statistic is 4.035 (3.053/.757), with significance level of .019. Hence, although the means appear quite similar, there is statistical difference, and we conclude that the repurchase intention is affected by the income level. The post-hoc test examines which groups are different (Figure 3.13). We performed just one (Tukey) for illustrative purposes, but there are several options, and each one has a specific feature according to the data characteristics and assumptions violations (Hair, Anderson, Tatham, & Black, 2005). By the significance level, the difference lies between groups high and middle, which is explained by the descriptive. The highest repurchase intention comes from the high-income group and the lowest comes from the middle-income group.

	N	Mean	Std. Deviation	Std. Error	95% Confidence Interval for Mean Lower Bound	95% Confidence Interval for Mean Upper Bound	Minimum	Maximum
High	100	6.5500	.75712	.07571	6.3998	6.7002	4.00	7.00
Middle	100	6.2100	.89098	.08910	6.0332	6.3868	4.00	7.00
Low	100	6.3100	.95023	.09502	6.1215	6.4985	2.00	7.00
Total	300	6.3567	.87865	.05073	6.2568	6.4565	2.00	7.00

Figure 3.10 ANOVA, output, I.

		Levene Statistic	df1	df2	Sig.
repurchase intention	Based on Mean	3.357	2	297	.036
	Based on Median	4.329	2	297	.014
	Based on Median and with Adjusted *df*	4.329	2	248.116	.014
	Based on Trimmed Mean	4.251	2	297	.015

Figure 3.11 ANOVA, output, II.

	Sum of Squares	df	Mean Square	F	Sig.
Between Groups	6.107	2	3.053	4.035	.019
Within Groups	224.730	297	.757		
Total	230.837	299			

Figure 3.12 ANOVA, output, III.

(I) Type	(J) Type	Mean Difference (I-J)	Std. Error	Sig.	95% Confidence Interval Lower Bound	95% Confidence Interval Upper Bound
high	Middle	.34000*	.12302	.017	.0502	.6298
	Low	.24000	.12302	.126	−.0498	.5298
middle	High	−.34000*	.12302	.017	−.6298	−.0502
	Low	−.10000	.12302	.695	−.3898	.1898
low	High	−.24000	.12302	.126	−.5298	.0498
	Middle	.10000	.12302	.695	−.1898	.3898

* The mean difference is significant at the 0.05 level.

Figure 3.13 ANOVA, output, IV.

Interaction effects

Sometimes, the difference between parameters may be caused by a third variable, a demographic characteristic, for example. To identify this possible effect, we may test the interaction effect. Let's verify if gender interacts with income in causing effects on loyalty. Testing interaction effects requires a different procedure in SPSS. The steps are:

1   Analyze;
2   General Linear Models;
3   Univariate;
4   Select Variables;

    a   Select Dependent variable (here: repurchase intention);
    b   Select Fixed Factors (here: income type, gender);

5   Select Plots

    a   The independent variable (here: income type) on the Horizontal Axis;
    b   The interaction effect (here: gender) as Separate Lines;
    c   Select "Add";
    d   Continue;

6   Select Post-Hoc;

    a   Select Factors (here: income type, gender);
    b   Select Tukey;
    c   Continue;

7   Select EM Means (Univariate Estimated Marginal Means);

    a   Select all variables, check compare main effects, then Continue;

8   Select Options;

    a   Select Descriptives;
    b   Select Homogeneity tests;
    c   Select Estimates of effect size;
    d   Continue;

9   OK

Figure 3.14 ANOVA with interaction effects, I.

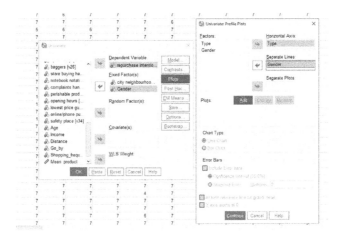

Figure 3.15 ANOVA with interaction effects, II.

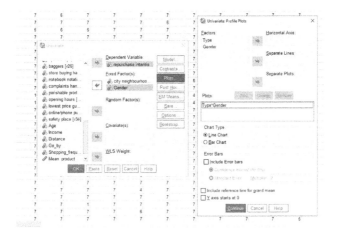

Figure 3.16 ANOVA with interaction effects, III.

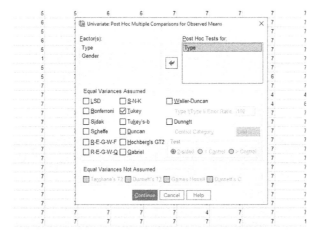

Figure 3.17 ANOVA with interaction effects, IV.

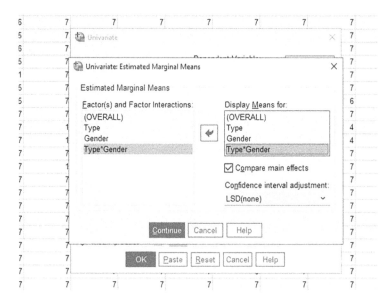

Figure 3.18 ANOVA with interaction effects, V.

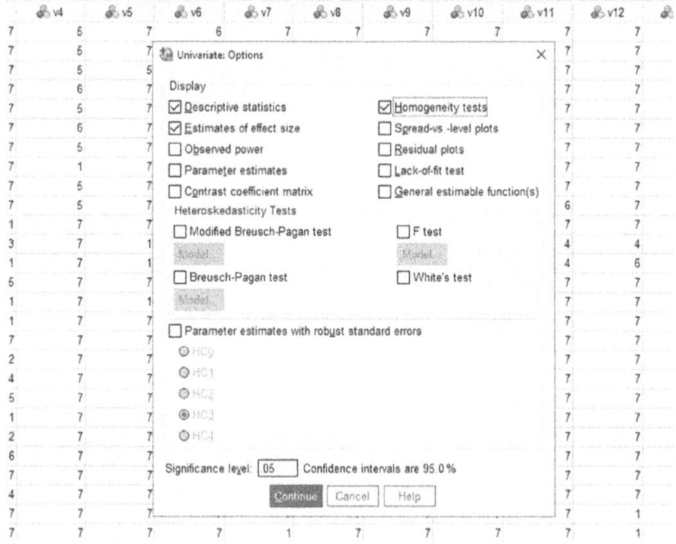

Figure 3.19 ANOVA with interaction effects, VI.

The first outcome is the table with the descriptive statistics (Figure 3.20). It has now six different groups, divided by income and gender. As in the previous example, the means seem to be not so different, although in all income groups, women present higher repurchase intention in each group. The test of homogeneity of variance (Figure 3.21) is now significative, but we disregard this violation, because it has no serious effects when the groups are the same size (Hair et al., 2005; Sharma, 1996). Figure 3.22 shows the between-subject effects. The significance level indicates that only the variable "type" (income, sig = .025) influences the repurchase intention; neither the gender nor the interaction cause effect. The pairwise comparisons (Figures 3.23 and 3.24) confirm the results, showing differences only between high and middle income (sig = .010). The estimated Marginal Means Graph (Figure 3.25) summarizes all the tests, showing the same pattern for males and females. The conclusion of this analysis is that the interaction effect of gender is not significant.

Type	Gender	Mean	Std. Deviation	N
high	1.00	6.3902	.89101	41
	2.00	6.6610	.63273	59
	Total	6.5500	.75712	100
middle	1.00	6.1579	.82286	38
	2.00	6.2419	.93538	62
	Total	6.2100	.89098	100
low	1.00	6.1563	.88388	32
	2.00	6.3824	.97780	68
	Total	6.3100	.95023	100
Total	1.00	6.2432	.86567	111
	2.00	6.4233	.88166	189
	Total	6.3567	.87865	300

Figure 3.20 ANOVA with interaction effects, output, I.

Levene's Test of Equality of Error Variances[a,b]

		Levene Statistic	df1	df2	Sig.
repurchase intention	Based on Mean	2.864	5	294	.015
	Based on Median	1.827	5	294	.107
	Based on Median and with adjusted df	1.827	5	248.097	.108
	Based on trimmed mean	3.084	5	294	.010

Note: Tests the null hypothesis that the error variance of the dependent variable is equal across groups.
a. Dependent variable: repurchase intention.
b. Design: Intercept + Type + Gender + Type × Gender.

Figure 3.21 ANOVA with interaction effects, output, II.

Source	Type III Sum of Squares	df	Mean Square	F	Sig.	Partial Eta Squared
Corrected Model	9.159[a]	5	1.832	2.429	.035	.040
Intercept	11123.907	1	11123.907	14753.086	.000	.980
Type	5.612	2	2.806	3.721	.025	.025
Gender	2.601	1	2.601	3.450	.064	.012
Type * Gender	.450	2	.225	.298	.742	.002
Error	221.678	294	.754			
Total	12353.000	300				
Corrected Total	230.837	299				

a. R-squared = .040 (Adjusted R-squared = .023).

Figure 3.22 ANOVA with interaction effects, output, III.

| | | | | | 95% Confidence Interval for Difference[b] | |
(I) Type	(J) Type	Mean Difference (I-J)	Std. Error	Sig.[b]	Lower Bound	Upper Bound
high	middle	.326*	.126	.010	.078	.573
	low	.256*	.128	.047	.004	.509
middle	high	−.326*	.126	.010	−.573	−.078
	low	−.069	.129	.591	−.323	.185
low	high	−.256*	.128	.047	−.509	−.004
	middle	.069	.129	.591	−.185	.323

Note: Based on estimated marginal means.
* The mean difference is significant at the .05 level.
b. Adjustment for multiple comparisons: least significant difference (equivalent to no adjustments).

Figure 3.23 ANOVA with interaction effects, output, IV.

| | | Mean Difference (I-J) | | | 95% Confidence Interval for Difference[a] | |
(I) GENDER	(J) GENDER		Std. Error	Sig.[a]	Lower Bound	Upper Bound
1.00	2.00	−.194	.104	.064	−.399	.012
2.00	1.00	.194	.104	.064	−.012	.399

Note: Based on estimated marginal means.
a. Adjustment for multiple comparisons: least significant difference (equivalent to no adjustments).

Figure 3.24 ANOVA with interaction effects, output, V.

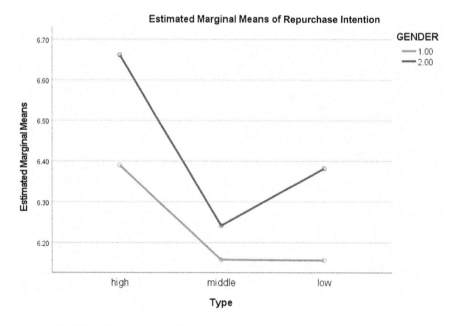

Figure 3.25 ANOVA with interaction effects, output, VI.

3.5 Theoretical background – multivariate analysis of variance (MANOVA)

There are cases in which the objective is to evaluate the differences between groups of more than one dependent variable. As an illustration, imagine a survey whose objective is to assess whether the categorical independent variable – with 3 treatments, low, middle, and high income – influences not only the store loyalty but also the satisfaction – both metric dependent variables. Another example would be to test whether there are differences in wearing fashionable clothes and in spending money on fashion, depending on marital status (single, married, divorced, and widowed). In both cases, there is more than one metric dependent variable for one, or more than one, categorical independent variable. Graphically, the situation would be as illustrated in Figure 3.26.

In this case, we intend to evaluate the effect of the categorical variable on the dependent variables simultaneously, which is quite different from the univariate evaluation, which would consider each dependent variable separately. In other words, two variables may present statistically significant differences in univariate terms, but the same may not occur in multivariate terms.

The explanation for this stems from the geometric space under consideration. Intuitively, one can think of a practical explanation. Imagine a classroom with a table in front of the blackboard. Two objects placed on the table, each one at an opposite end, would be considered distant, considering only the table area. Considering the entire classroom, these same two objects are very close.

Therefore, MANOVA is a technique used to assess the statistical significance of the difference between groups, according to the function:

$$Y_1 + Y_2 + Y_3 + \ldots + Y_n = X_1 + X_2 + X_3 + \ldots + X_k$$

Where:
Y_1, Y_2, Y_3, Y_n are the dependent metric variables;
X, X, X_3, X_k are the nonmetric independent variables.

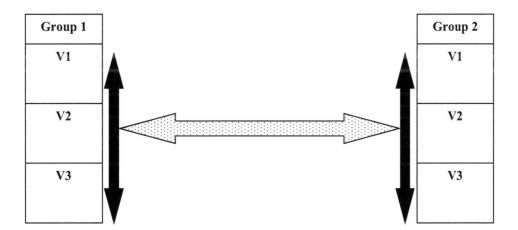

Figure 3.26 MANOVA: Variance within group versus variance between groups.

The tested null hypothesis is the equality of the vectors of the means of multiple groups of dependent variables.

$$H_0 = \begin{pmatrix} \mu_{11} \\ \mu_{21} \\ \mu_{31} \\ \vdots \\ \mu_{n1} \end{pmatrix} = \begin{pmatrix} \mu_{12} \\ \mu_{22} \\ \mu_{32} \\ \vdots \\ \mu_{n2} \end{pmatrix} = \cdots = \begin{pmatrix} \mu_{1k} \\ \mu_{2k} \\ \mu_{3k} \\ \vdots \\ \mu_{nk} \end{pmatrix}$$

Wherein:

μ_{ij} is the mean of the i_{th} variable for the j_{th} group.

The alternative hypothesis would be that at least one vector of means is different.

Several multivariate significance tests have been proposed, with emphasis on Pillai's Trace, Hotelling's Trace, Wilks' Lambda and Roy's Largest Root. In the case of a two-group MANOVA, Hotelling's T2 can be calculated, based on the squared Mahalanobis distance and its transformation into F statistics (Sharma, 1996). The formulas are presented here.

T² de Hotelling: $T^2 = \left(\dfrac{n_1 \times n_2}{n_1 + n_2} \right) MD^2$

$$F = \frac{(n_1 + n_2 - p - 1)}{(n_1 + n_2 - p)2} T^2$$

Pillai's Trace: $PT = \displaystyle\sum_{i=1}^{k} \frac{\lambda_i}{1 + \lambda_i}$

Hotelling's Trace: $HT = \displaystyle\sum_{i=1}^{k} \lambda_i$

Wilks' Λ: $W\Lambda = \displaystyle\prod_{i=1}^{k} \frac{1}{1 + \lambda_i}$

Roy's Largest Root: $RLR = \dfrac{\lambda_{max}}{1 + \lambda_{max}}$

Wherein:

λ_i is the highest eigenvalue (refers to the sum of squares and cross products of the variation matrices within and between groups).

k is the number of eigenvalues.

After performing the multivariate test, the univariate test should be performed, to identify which dependent variables may be statistically different. It should be noted that the purpose of this test is precisely to identify possible similarities between means of variables that were not identified in the multivariate test.

In addition to univariate tests, it is also important to perform the so-called post hoc tests, which aim to identify differences between groups or independent categorical variables. In other words, when a difference was found by the multivariate test, the question remains: which groups differ from each other? Post hoc tests are used for this purpose.

The most common post hoc tests are the Scheffé method, Tukey's HSD (honestly significant difference) method, Fisher's LSD (least significant difference) method, Duncan's multiple amplitude test, and Newman–Kuels test (Hair et al., 2005).

However, they all have problems with test power and therefore should be used with caution. The authors also emphasize that the most conservative method, regarding the type I error, is that of Scheffé, followed by HSD, LSD, Newman–Kuels, and Duncan.

Some assumptions must be checked beforehand, as their violation can have an effect on the properties of statistical tests. In addition to verifying the data normality, it should be tested whether the variance-covariance matrix is equivalent (homoscedasticity).

Univariate normality is assessed by Kolmogorov–Smirnov and Shapiro–Wilks tests, in addition to kurtosis and skewness statistics. SPSS does not have a specific test for multivariate normality, but if all variables show univariate normality, even if multivariate normality is not obtained, the effect of the violation would be small, or even nonexistent.

The equality of the variance-covariance matrix can be verified by the Box M test, with the aid of the Levene test, for each variable individually. Often, the multivariate violation is due to data non-normality, which leads to the conclusion that correcting one can correct the other violation. Furthermore, the violation is also of little importance when it comes to samples of equal sizes for each group.

3.6 Application of MANOVA in SPSS

To illustrate, we will use the database referring to the survey with supermarket customers. Let's assess if income influences customers' evaluation of retail store features. The independent categorical variable is the income level, with three categories, high, middle, and low. The dependent variables are:

v4: fast checkout;
v8: product quality;
v13: parking lot.

The steps are:

1   Analyze;
2   General Linear Models;
3   Multivariate;
4   Select Variables;

   a   Select Dependent variables (here: fast checkout (v4), product quality (v8), and parking lot (v13));
   b   Select Fixed Factors (here: income type);

5   Select Post-Hoc;

   a   Select Factors (here: income type);
   b   Select Tukey;
   c   Continue;

6   Select Options;

   a   Select Descriptive statistics;
   b   Select Observed power;

  c Select Homogeneity tests;
  d Continue;

7 OK

Readers workshop

a Open the supermarket database;
b Perform the analysis, following the steps listed;
c Analyze the descriptive;
d Check the data homoscedasticity;
e Test if income has effect on the combination of fast checkout, product quality, and parking lot;
f Test on which dependent variable (fast checkout, product quality, and parking lot) income has effect;
g Test which income levels have effect on each dependent variable (fast checkout, product quality, and parking lot) separately.

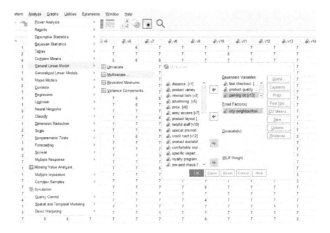

Figure 3.27 MANOVA, I.

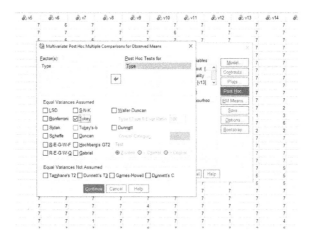

Figure 3.28 MANOVA, II.

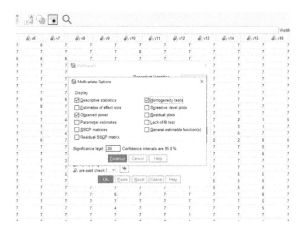

Figure 3.29 MANOVA, III.

The first outcome is shown in Figure 3.30, with means and standard deviations for the variables and groups. Parking lot has the lowest ratings, while product quality has the highest and is more homogeneous. The Box's Test shows different variance across groups, violating the assumption and we already know the variables did not achieve univariate normality. Due to the equal groups size and the simple size, we continue with the analysis.

	Type	Mean	Std. Deviation	N
fast checkout	high	6.1900	1.23660	100
	middle	5.5200	1.61107	100
	low	5.8600	1.27144	100
	Total	5.8567	1.40572	300
product quality	high	6.7300	.72272	100
	middle	6.5000	.81029	100
	low	6.4100	1.02588	100
	Total	6.5467	.87006	300
parking lot	high	5.3700	2.16331	100
	middle	3.7300	2.64329	100
	low	3.2700	2.58142	100
	Total	4.1233	2.62381	300

Figure 3.30 MANOVA, output, I.

Box's Test of Equality of Covariance Matrices[a]

Box's M		41.981
F		3.447
*df*1		12
*df*2		427474.385
Sig.		.000

Note: Tests the null hypothesis that the observed covariance matrices of the dependent variables are equal across groups.
a. Design: Intercept + Type

Figure 3.31 MANOVA, output, II.

All the multivariate tests (see Figure 3.32) show significant differences (.000), confirming the influence of income on the combination of dependent variables. It means that the evaluation customers make about the three variables is different for different income levels.

Effect		Value	F	Hypothesis df	Error df	Sig.	Noncent. Parameter	Observed Power[d]
Multivariate Tests[a]								
Intercept	Pillai's Trace	.984	6146.212[b]	3.000	295.000	.000	18438.635	1.000
	Wilks' Lambda	.016	6146.212[b]	3.000	295.000	.000	18438.635	1.000
	Hotelling's Trace	62.504	6146.212[b]	3.000	295.000	.000	18438.635	1.000
	Roy's Largest Root	62.504	6146.212[b]	3.000	295.000	.000	18438.635	1.000
Type	Pillai's Trace	.149	7.917	6.000	592.000	.000	47.501	1.000
	Wilks' Lambda	.854	8.066[b]	6.000	590.000	.000	48.399	1.000
	Hotelling's Trace	.168	8.215	6.000	588.000	.000	49.292	1.000
	Roy's Largest Root	.146	14.427[c]	3.000	296.000	.000	43.282	1.000

a. Design: Intercept + Type.
b. Exact statistic.
c. The statistic is an upper bound on F that yields a lower bound on the significance level.
d. Computed using alpha = .05.

Figure 3.32 MANOVA, output, III.

Figure 3.33 shows the univariate tests. The significance levels (.003, .027, and .000) show the difference between the three variables, thus confirming that customers with different income evaluate each variable differently.

Source	Dependent Variable	Type III Sum of Squares	df	Mean Square	F	Sig.	Noncent. Parameter	Observed Power[d]
Corrected Model	fast checkout	22.447[a]	2	11.223	5.865	.003	11.729	.872
	product quality	5.447[b]	2	2.723	3.662	.027	7.323	.672
	parking lot	243.707[c]	2	121.853	19.943	.000	39.885	1.000
Intercept	fast checkout	10290.163	1	10290.163	5376.904	.000	5376.904	1.000
	product quality	12857.653	1	12857.653	17287.112	.000	17287.112	1.000
	parking lot	5100.563	1	5100.563	834.762	.000	834.762	1.000
Type	fast checkout	22.447	2	11.223	5.865	.003	11.729	.872
	product quality	5.447	2	2.723	3.662	.027	7.323	.672
	parking lot	243.707	2	121.853	19.943	.000	39.885	1.000
Error	fast checkout	568.390	297	1.914				
	product quality	220.900	297	.744				
	parking lot	1814.730	297	6.110				
Total	fast checkout	10881.000	300					
	product quality	13084.000	300					
	parking lot	7159.000	300					

Figure 3.33 MANOVA, output, IV.

Source	Dependent Variable	Type III Sum of Squares	df	Mean Square	F	Sig.	Noncent. Parameter	Observed Power[d]
Corrected Total	fast checkout	590.837	299					
	product quality	226.347	299					
	parking lot	2058.437	299					

a. R-squared = .038 (adjusted R-squared = .032).
b. R-squared = .024 (adjusted R-squared = .017).
c. R-squared = .118 (adjusted R-squared = .112).
d. Computed using alpha = .05.

Figure 3.33 (Continued)

Finally, we see in Figure 3.34 the difference between groups in each variable. Concerning fast checkout, the difference lies between high and middle. In the case of product quality, there is difference between high and low, and for parking lot, between high and middle, and high and low. Turning back to Figure 3.30, we observe the greatest ratings come from the high-income group for all variables, associated with the lowest standard deviations.

Dependent Variable	(I) Type	(J) Type	Mean Difference (I–J)	Std. Error	Sig.	95% Confidence Interval Lower Bound	95% Confidence Interval Upper Bound
fast checkout	high	middle	.6700*	.19564	.002	.2092	1.1308
		low	.3300	.19564	.212	−.1308	.7908
	middle	high	−.6700*	.19564	.002	−1.1308	−.2092
		low	−.3400	.19564	.193	−.8008	.1208
	low	high	−.3300	.19564	.212	−.7908	.1308
		middle	.3400	.19564	.193	−.1208	.8008
product quality	high	middle	.2300	.12196	.145	−.0573	.5173
		low	.3200*	.12196	.025	.0327	.6073
	middle	high	−.2300	.12196	.145	−.5173	.0573
		low	.0900	.12196	.741	−.1973	.3773
	low	high	−.3200*	.12196	.025	−.6073	−.0327
		middle	−.0900	.12196	.741	−.3773	.1973
parking lot	high	middle	1.6400*	.34958	.000	.8166	2.4634
		low	2.1000*	.34958	.000	1.2766	2.9234
	middle	high	−1.6400*	.34958	.000	−2.4634	−.8166
		low	.4600	.34958	.387	−.3634	1.2834
	low	high	−2.1000*	.34958	.000	−2.9234	−1.2766
		middle	−.4600	.34958	.387	−1.2834	.3634

Note: Based on observed means. The error term is Mean Square (Error) = 6.110.
* The mean difference is significant at the .05 level.

Figure 3.34 MANOVA, output, V.

Exercise

A manufacturer of high-end fashion, concerned about the growth in the sale of counterfeit goods, conducted a survey to assess the relationship between income and purchase of these products. The purchase behavior was measured using a seven-point interval scale, ranging from (1) never to (7) frequently, and the income was measured in three groups, low, middle, and high. The figures that follow present the ANOVA results.

	N	Mean	Std. Deviation	Std. Error	95% Confidence Interval for Mean		Minimum	Maximum
					Lower Bound	Upper Bound		
Low	105	4.1143	1.72824	.16866	3.7798	4.4487	1.00	7.00
Middle	146	3.6644	1.62853	.13478	3.3980	3.9308	1.00	7.00
High	58	3.0172	1.42030	.18649	2.6438	3.3907	1.00	6.00
Total	309	3.6958	1.66652	.09480	3.5092	3.8823	1.00	7.00

Figure 3.35 Exercise, I.

		Levene Statistic	df1	df2	Sig.
Purchase	Based on Mean	1.790	2	306	.169
	Based on Median	1.378	2	306	.254
	Based on Median and with Adjusted *df*	1.378	2	300.737	.254
	Based on Trimmed Mean	1.706	2	306	.183

Figure 3.36 Exercise, II.

	Sum of Squares	df	Mean Square	F	Sig.
Between Groups	45.238	2	22.619	8.543	.000
Within Groups	810.166	306	2.648		
Total	855.405	308			

Figure 3.37 Exercise, III.

(I) Income_ Group	(J) Income_ Group	Mean Difference (I-J)	Std. Error	Sig.	95% Confidence Interval	
					Lower Bound	Upper Bound
Low	Middle	.44990	.20821	.080	−.0405	.9403
	High	1.09704*	.26620	.000	.4701	1.7240
Middle	Low	−.44990	.20821	.080	−.9403	.0405
	High	.64714*	.25255	.029	.0523	1.2419
High	Low	−1.09704*	.26620	.000	−1.7240	−.4701
	Middle	−.64714*	.25255	.029	−1.2419	−.0523

* The mean difference is significant at the 0.05 level.

Figure 3.38 Exercise, IV.

Questions

1   Do the groups present equivalent variances?
2   Is the purchase behavior different between the income groups?
3   Which groups present different purchase behavior?
4   Based on the ANOVA results, which conclusions can you give to the fashion manufacturer?

Market insight

Several companies provide Customer Service in order to support customers before and after they purchase and use products and services. Normally, companies ask customer to evaluate the support they received, answering questions such as:

- *What is your satisfaction with the associate that helped you?*
- *What is your satisfaction with the solution the company offered?*
- *Was your problem totally fixed?*
- *What is your satisfaction with the support process?*
- *What is your intention to remain as our client?*
- *What is the likelihood of recommending the company to friends and relatives?*

How can ANOVA/MANOVA be used to gather information from customers with different demographic profiles?

Suggested readings

Bhattacharjee, A., & Mogilner, C. (2014). Happiness from ordinary and extraordinary experiences. *Journal of Consumer Research, 41*(1), 1–17.

Bian, Q., & Forsythe, S. (2012). Purchase intention for luxury brands: A cross cultural comparison. *Journal of Business Research, 65*(10), 1443–1451.

Hsee, C. K., Yang, Y., Li, N., & Shen, L. (2009). Wealth, warmth, and well-being: Whether happiness is relative or absolute depends on whether it is about money, acquisition, or consumption. *Journal of Marketing Research, 46*(3), 396–409.

Leng, C. Y., & Botelho, D. (2010). How does national culture impact on consumers decision-making styles? A cross cultural study in Brazil, the United States and Japan. *BAR–Brazilian Administration Review, 7*(3), 260–275.

Nicolao, L., Irwin, J. R., & Goodman, J. K. (2009). Happiness for sale: Do experiential purchases make consumers happier than material purchases? *Journal of Consumer Research, 36*(2), 188–198.

Zampetakis, L. A. (2014). The emotional dimension of the consumption of luxury counterfeit goods: An empirical taxonomy. *Marketing Intelligence & Planning, 32*(1), 21–40.

4 Regression analysis

Simple regression analysis is a statistical technique used to analyze the relationship between two metric variables, a dependent (or explained) variable and one independent (or explanatory) variable. When it comes to the relationship between a dependent and more than one independent variable, it is called multiple regression analysis. It is probably the best-known and most used technique among multivariate statistical techniques.

Regression serves the purpose of measuring the effects of independent variables on the dependent variable. For example, if the price of a product or service changes, what will the change in sales be? What is the effect of promotion on sales? What are the most important variables explaining customer loyalty?

In all these examples, we must assess the impact of one or more metric independent variables on a (metric) dependent variable. The use of the regression analysis requires, first of all, the choice of a theoretical model to be tested, in addition to the choice of variables. The sample should have at least five observations for each independent variable included in the model, but the ideal is between 15 and 20.

The theoretical background of simple and multiple regression analysis are explained in sections 4.1 and 4.2, respectively. Section 4.3 gives examples for marketing application, and section 4.4 discusses the application of multiple regression in IBM SPSS Statistics Software (SPSS).

4.1 Theoretical background – simple regression analysis

The simple regression model can be presented as follows:

$$Y_i = \beta_0 + \beta_1 X_i + \varepsilon_i$$

Where:
Y_i is the dependent variable;
X_i is the independent variable;
β_0 is the intercept of the regression equation, which indicates the average value of the dependent variable when the independent is equal to zero (point where the regression line crosses the Y axis);
β_1 is the regression coefficient, which shows the regression line slope and measures the expected change in the mean value of the dependent variable when the independent variable varies by one;
ε_i is the random error (residual) or stochastic disturbance, representing the difference between the observed value and the estimated value of the dependent variable.

DOI: 10.4324/9781003196617-4

As it is a stochastic relationship, the values of Y can never be predicted exactly based on the values of X, but simply estimated, given the presence of the random error. Thus, some considerations regarding the error term/residuals must be made, the so-called basic assumptions:

1 Normality: the error term/residual ε_i has a normal probability distribution;
2 The average of the error terms/residuals is zero: $E(\varepsilon_i) = 0$;
3 Homoscedasticity: the error variance is the same for all observations, $E(\varepsilon_i)^2 = \sigma^2$;
4 Independence of the error terms/residuals: the error of one period does not affect the error of the subsequent period(s), $E(\varepsilon_i \varepsilon_j) = 0$.

Several methods can be used to calculate β_0 and β_1, the most common being ordinary least squares, which consists of minimizing the sum of the squared deviations of the observed values in relation to the estimated values, or

$$\Sigma \hat{u}_i^2 = \Sigma \left(Y_i - \hat{Y}_i \right)^2 = \Sigma \left(Y_i - \hat{\beta}_0 - \hat{\beta}_1 \right)^2$$

$$\hat{\beta}_1 = \Sigma \left(X_i - \bar{X} \right) \left(Y_i - \bar{Y} \right)$$

$$\hat{\beta}_0 = \bar{Y} - \hat{B}\bar{X}$$

In this way, what is intended is to estimate a line that passes as close as possible to the observed points. Graphically, the situation would be like the one in Figure 4.1. Considering the difference between the observed point (Y_i) and the estimated point $(\hat{Y}_i)$, the solution is reached when the sum of the squared deviations is minimal.

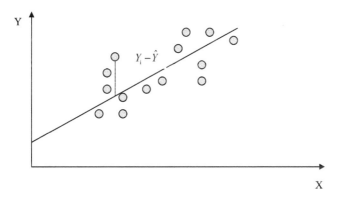

Figure 4.1 Regression line.

In this case, least squares estimators have the following properties:

1 They are not biased; that is, they correspond to the true values of β_0 and β_1;
2 They are efficient, which means that they have minimal variance;
3 They are consistent, or asymptotically non-biased;
4 They are asymptotically efficient.

Items 3 and 4 imply that the properties remain when the sample size increases.

Variance decomposition

When X varies, it causes variations in Y, but how much of the variance in Y can be attributed to the variance in X? To make such a measurement, the analysis of variance should be used. The total variance of Y in relation to its mean is given by the total sum of squares, SS_{total}, or

$$SS_t = \left(Y_i - \bar{Y}\right)^2$$

It is important to determine how much of SS_{total} can be attributed to X and how much is due to random factors, not included in the model.

The regression sum of squares (SS_r), which is the squared difference between the observed values and the mean, indicates the variance explained by the independent variable X. The error sum of squares (SS_e), or the sum of the squared differences between the observed value and the estimated value, indicates the unexplained variation, due to random causes:

$$SS_r = \Sigma\left(\hat{Y}_i - \bar{Y}\right)^2$$

$$SS_e = \Sigma\left(Y_i - \hat{Y}_i\right)^2 = \Sigma\left(e_i\right)^2$$

In this way, dividing the explained variance, SS_r, by the Y total variance, SS_t, we obtain the coefficient of determination, R^2, which measures the fit between the regression line and the observed data, that is, it indicates the proportion of variance in Y that can be attributed to variance in the independent variable X.

$$R^2 = \frac{SS_r}{SS_t}$$

Note that $0 \leq R^2 \leq 1$

Hypothesis testing

If the independent variable has no influence on the dependent, the regression line would be parallel to the horizontal axis, and B_1 would be statistically equal to zero.

Because of this, to assess the importance of the independent variable to explain the dependent variable, one can resort to the development of hypothesis tests, testing: $H_0: \beta = 0$, against $H_1: \beta \neq 0$.

4.2 Theoretical background – multiple regression analysis

The multiple regression analysis is a model that includes more than one independent variable, according to the following equation:

$$Y_i = \beta_o + \beta_1 X_{i1} + \beta_2 X_{i2} + \ldots + \beta_k X_{ik} + \varepsilon_i$$

It is a natural extension of the simple regression analysis. In this way, most of the results derived from a simple regression can be generalized to multiple regression (Kmenta, 1997). Concerning the assumptions, those regarding normality, error zero mean, homoscedasticity, and independence of error terms prevail. An additional assumption is that there is no exact linear relationship between the independent variables.

The meaning of the regression coefficients becomes a little different. Each regression coefficient symbolizes the change in the dependent variable, given a unitary change in the k_{th} independent variable, keeping the other independent variables constant. As such, they represent partial regression coefficients. Since most social sciences experiments are uncontrolled, it is impossible to keep the other independent variables constant. Consequently, we must consider the regression "net effect" on the dependent variable, discounting the combined effect of the other independent variables.

It is also important to check the number of observations and independent variables. Normally, the coefficient of determination increases with an increase in the number of observations (n) or the number of variables (k), even when the variable does not have much importance in the model. Consequently, to assess the degree of fit between the estimated function and the observed values, one should resort to the adjusted coefficient of determination, calculated in the following way:

$$\bar{R}^2 = R^2 - \frac{k-1}{n-k}\left(1-R^2\right)$$

It should be noted that the adjusted coefficient of determination can be smaller than zero and will always maintain the following relationship: $\bar{R}^2 \leq R^2$.

To test whether none of the independent variables has an influence on the dependent variable, a broader test can be used, evaluating $H_0: \beta_1 = \beta_2 = \ldots = \beta_k = 0$, against the alternative hypothesis that H_0 is false. If H_0 is true, the variance of the dependent variable will be affected only by the random error, and therefore $SS_r = 0$ and SS_t will equal SS_e.

The appropriate statistic test is:

$$\frac{SS_r\big/ k-1}{SS_e \big/ n-k} \approx F_{k-1,n-k}$$

Wherein $F_{k-1, n-k}$ represents the F distribution, with $k-1$ degrees of freedom in the numerator and $n-k$ in the denominator. If the test statistic is not significantly different from zero, there will be no influence of the independent variables on the dependent one.

The assumptions of multiple regression

As mentioned before, the following assumptions must be met in multiple regression:

- Normality;
- Average of the error terms (residuals) is zero;
- Homoscedasticity;
- Independence of error terms (residuals);
- No exact linear relationship between the independent variables.

These assumptions are not always verified. The first two do not cause major problems as long as the sample is large, according to Kmenta (1997) and Damodar (2004). The other three assumptions, however, deserve special attention.

Assumption of homoscedasticity

The assumption of homoscedasticity implies that the error variance is the same for all observations, $E(\varepsilon_i)^2 = \sigma^2$. When this does not occur, that is, when the variance of the random error is not the same for all observations, there is heteroscedasticity; this is common in cross-section data. For example, when studying household spending on food in relation to income, it is quite normal that high incomes families' spending is more dispersed than low-income families spending.

When heteroscedasticity occurs, the least squares estimators remain non-biased and efficient but are no longer asymptotically non-biased and asymptotically efficient; that is, they lose the properties of large samples. The problem arises in the construction of confidence intervals and the development of hypotheses tests, since the confidence intervals and the acceptance regions may be narrower or wider than the correct ones.

To identify a heteroscedastic series, a simple regression for each of the independent variables can be performed, plotting the residuals. If they show variations in a systematic way, the series should be heteroscedastic. Figure 4.2 shows the scatterplot of a heteroscedastic series. As the income increases, the residuals dispersion also increases.

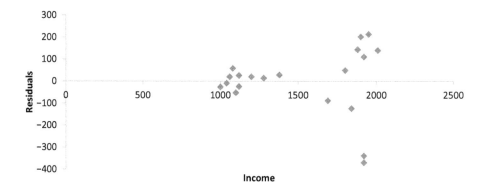

Figure 4.2 Income residual plot.

The Goldfeld Quandt test can also be used, according to the following procedure: set the data in ascending order (if any), split the sample into two, not necessarily the same size, and run one regression for each. Then estimate the ratio between the residual mean square of each regression.

$$H_0 = \sigma_1^2 = \sigma_2^2 \qquad H_1 = \sigma_1^2 \neq \sigma_2^2 \qquad GQ = \frac{\sigma_1^2}{\sigma_2^2} \sim F_{n_1-k_1, n_2-k_2}$$

Check the result following the F test. If H_0 is accepted, the series will be homoscedastic, but if heteroscedasticity is detected, a correction procedure is needed. For this purpose, the observations of each subsample can be divided by the respective standard error. This creates a new series, probably homoscedastic, but it is convenient to double check. In addition, when the sample and the type of analysis allow, one can work with only the results found in each subsample.

Independence of the error terms

By the assumption $E(\varepsilon_i \varepsilon_j) = 0$, the error of one period does not affect the error of the other period. When this does not occur, the model is autoregressive. This means that there is autocorrelation: the error of one period is correlated with the error of other period(s).

Table 4.1 Durbin–Watson test; intervals for acceptance or rejection of $d = 0$

$H_0: d = 0$ versus $H_1 d > 0*$	$H_0: d = 0$ versus $H_1 d \neq 0*$
Rejection if $d < d_L$	Rejection if $d < d_L$ or if $d > 4 - d_L$
No rejection if $d > d_U$	No rejection if $d_U < d < 4 - d_U$
Inconclusive test if $d_L < d < d_U$	Inconclusive test $d_L < d < d_U$ or $4 - d_U < d < 4 - d_L$

Source: Kmenta (1997).
* d_L and d_U values can be found in Durbin–Watson Table (L = lower, U = upper)

Autocorrelation is common in time series, with a higher probability for shorter time intervals, that is, it is more likely for monthly than annual data, for example.

There is autocorrelation, for instance, in a situation where the sales of ice cream today are higher than expected by the regression model, and then also tomorrow there is a higher probability of selling unexpected more ice cream. Autocorrelation can be caused by the absence of relevant independent variables. For instance, the independent variable "temperature" could have been forgotten in the ice cream sales model: more ice cream is consumed on warmer days, and above-average temperatures generally happen in series of several days in a row.

In this case, too, least squares estimators are not efficient and asymptotically efficient, but they maintain the properties of non-biased and consistent. As with the violation of the homoscedasticity assumption, problems arise with the construction of confidence intervals and the development of hypothesis tests, since the confidence intervals and the acceptance regions may be narrower or wider than the correct ones.

To identify an autoregressive model (autocorrelation), we can use the Durbin–Watson test, which consists of testing whether the statistic $d = 0$, as shown below. The criterion for acceptance or rejection is shown in Table 4.1.

$$d = \frac{\sum_{t=2}^{n} (e_t - e_{t-1})^2}{\sum_{t=1}^{n} e_t^2}$$

If the model is autoregressive, it must be corrected, according to the Cochrane–Orcutt iterative method or the Durbin method. It should be noted that, in the case of inconclusive results, it is preferable to make the correction, because the non-correction of autoregressive data is more serious than the correction of non-autoregressive series (Johnston, 1972).

Multicollinearity

Independent variables cannot be perfectly correlated with any other independent variable or with any linear combination of independent variables. For example, if a retail store starts to charge for home delivery of purchases, which was free of charge before, customer evaluation on service quality, satisfaction, and loyalty probably will be affected simultaneously. When this occurs, there is multicollinearity.

If X_1 and X_2 are perfectly correlated, we can write: $X_1 = a + bX_2$
The least squares estimator is $\hat{\beta} = (X'X)^{-1}(X'Y)$
If there is a perfect correlation between the variables, the matrix $(X'X)$ is singular, and therefore its inverse does not exist. In this way, the solution to $\hat{\beta}$ is undetermined.

This is the extreme case of perfect multicollinearity. The most common, however, is that there is some degree of multicollinearity due to the types of data studied in social sciences, which do not come from controlled experiments, and therefore changes in one variable usually cause changes in other variables. Therefore, the question is not whether or not multicollinearity exists but the degree of multicollinearity.

With multicollinearity, the least squares estimators maintain all desirable properties, but as the variances and covariance of the parameters are large, the coefficient estimates are highly inaccurate. To measure the degree of multicollinearity, we can analyze the correlation coefficient between the variables. If this is higher, in absolute value, than 0.8, or if the variation inflation factor (VIF) is higher than 10, there are signs of a strong linear association.

Qualitative variables

Sometimes, the dependent variable is influenced by qualitative independent variables whose presence can be identified, but they are not measurable. In such cases, the regression analysis can include one or more qualitative variables.

Dummy variables

Also called binary or dichotomous variables, dummy variables represent qualitative characteristics of individuals or phenomena: characteristics that cannot be measured but simply observed regarding their presence or absence. Normally, a value of 1 is assigned for presence and 0 for absence. Take as an example the consumption of a certain product with seasonal characteristics, such as "tourist packages." In holiday months, the demand for tourist packages increases, despite the price rising. In the holiday period, there is a shift in the demand curve, a variation not captured by the regression model. To correct this problem, we can try to include a dummy variable. In this case, that would be the dummy variable "holiday period."

Trend variables

We often observe that changes of the dependent variable over time cannot be explained by the independent variables included in the model. Take as an example the consumption of processed foods over the past 50 years. Its growth cannot be credited only to changes in prices or income but mainly to changes in consumer habits. Since this habit change cannot be quantified, the inclusion of a trend variable can capture the effects of independent variables not included in the model. Normally, a value of 1 is used for the first observation and n for the last, or vice versa.

Binary dependent variables

There are times when the dependent variable cannot be quantified, representing only two options, such as going to work by car or bus, approving or not approving a particular government decision, liking a product or not, etc. In these cases, the dummy variable would be on the left side of the equation. This subject will be addressed in Chapter 6, "Discriminant Analysis."

Intrinsically linear models

On some occasions, despite some evidence to the contrary, the results of a regression model indicate a low degree of fit between the independent variables and the dependent variable. It may be that the observed points are not linear, although the variables are highly correlated.

Thus, the variation in size of the random error will give the false impression of low correlation between the variables. This situation occurs, for instance, in the relationship between spending on household food in relation to income, the change in agricultural production due to the application of fertilizers, the relationship between age and salary, and others.

Intrinsically linear models are nonlinear models with respect to variables but linear with respect to parameters. They can be converted into ordinary linear models through a convenient transformation of variables, such as inverse, squared root, squared, log.

4.3 Marketing application of regression analysis

A classic application of regression analysis is to evaluate changes in sales (demand) caused by a change in price or income, or both. This allows for estimation of the price elasticity of demand and income elasticity of demand, studies helpful in establishing price policy and product mix, respectively.

Advertising plays an important role in marketing, such as to increase sales, to strengthen the brand image, to increase awareness, etc. Regression analysis is useful in measuring the effects of advertising expenditures on performance-related variables such as sales. If a company launches a new marketing campaign, how much of the sales response could be attributed to it?

Internet and social media allowed customers to voice their opinions about products and services, what is called electronic word-of-mouth (e-WOM). As third party comments have great reliability, this became an important source of information for customers. Measuring the effects of e-WOM on performance variables such as sales, complaints, and profitability can help managers to improve results.

The presence of fans at sporting events may vary in relation to the weather, the team performance, the day of the week, the ticket price, etc. Which of them are able to fill the stadium? Likewise, which factors increase the popularity of music concerts, theater plays, or any artistic event?

Services have a peculiar feature due to the contact between employees and customers, the so-called moment of truth. In this sense, training and empowering employees becomes crucial to assure high service quality. What is the relationship between educational level, hours of training and capacity building, and leadership style on worker performance?

Among retail store attributes, there are many variables able to cause customer loyalty. Location, personnel, product variety, price, operating hours, and the presence of delivery service, are examples of a long list of possible influential variables. Thus, regression analysis is an important tool to identify which variables are most impactful in generating customer loyalty.

4.4 Application of multiple regression in SPSS

To illustrate the multiple regression analysis, we will use the supermarket database. The following variables will be used:
Dependent:

* v_{35}: repurchase intention.

Independent:

* v_4: fast check out.
* v_6: price.
* v_7: easy access.

- v_8: product quality.
- v_{24}: nearby convenience stores.

Multiple regression in SPSS requires the following steps to analyze these variables:

1 Analyze;
2 Regression;
3 Linear;
4 Select:

    a   Dependent: repurchase intention (v35);
    b   Independent(s): fast checkout (v4), price (v6), easy access (v7), product quality (v8), nearby convenience stores (v24);

5 Select Statistics;

    a   Choose Durbin–Watson;
    b   Choose Collinearity Diagnostics;
    c   Continue;

6 Select Plots:

    a   For Y: select DEPENDNT;
    b   For X: select *ZPRED;
    c   Choose Normal probability plot;
    d   Continue;

7 OK.

Readers workshop

a   Open the supermarket database;
b   Perform the analysis, following the steps listed;
c   Check the model explanatory power and significance;
d   Analyze each independent variable separately, based on relationship direction, coefficient value, and significance;
e   Check the error normality, homoscedasticity, and autoregression;
f   Analyze the results (what are the results' meaning?).

Figure 4.3 Multiple regression, I.

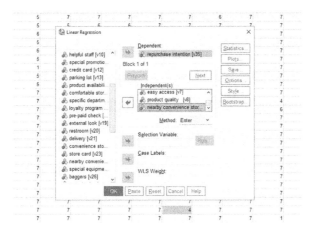

Figure 4.4 Multiple regression, II.

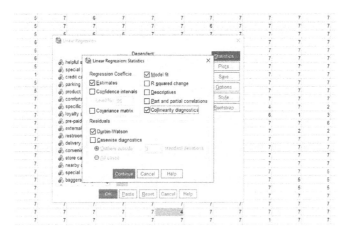

Figure 4.5 Multiple regression, III.

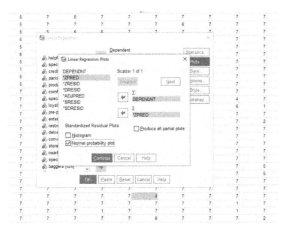

Figure 4.6 Multiple regression, IV.

The results will initially show the coefficient of determination (*R*-squared) and the adjusted coefficient of determination (adjusted *R*-squared) in the values of 0.250 and 0.238, respectively. Based on this information, we can say that almost 24% of the variation in the repurchase intention, the dependent variable, is explained by the independent variables together.

The ANOVA table (Figure 4.8) shows the *F* test. With a statistic of 19.649, the null hypothesis that SS_R is equal to zero is rejected at the significance level of 0.00. When the significance is lower than 0.050 (as is the case here), the independent variables, together, have a significant (important) impact on the dependent variable.

Figure 4.9 contains the coefficients non-standardized and standardized. It also shows the *t*-tests and the diagnosis of multicollinearity. According to the standardized data, the estimated equation is:

$$v_{35} = .260v_4 + .163v_6 + .108v_7 + .168v_8 + .064v_{24}.$$

Model Summary[b]

Model	R	R-Squared	Adjusted R-Squared	Std. Error of the Estimate	Durbin–Watson
1	.500[a]	.250	.238	.76714	1.596

a. Predictors: (Constant), nearby convenience stores, fast checkout, easy access, price, product quality.
b. Dependent Variable: repurchase intention.

Figure 4.7 Multiple regression, output, I.

ANOVA[a]

Model		Sum of Squares	df	Mean Square	F	Sig.
1	Regression	57.818	5	11.564	19.649	.000[b]
	Residual	173.019	294	.588		
	Total	230.837	299			

a. Dependent variable: repurchase intention.
b. Predictors: (Constant), nearby convenience stores, fast checkout, easy access, price, product quality.

Figure 4.8 Multiple regression, output, II.

Coefficients[a]

Model		Unstandardized Coefficients B	Unstandardized Coefficients Std. Error	Standardized Coefficients Beta	t	Sig.	Collinearity Statistics Tolerance	Collinearity Statistics VIF
1	(Constant)	2.603	.439		5.935	.000		
	fast checkout	.162	.037	.260	4.426	.000	.741	1.349
	price	.153	.053	.163	2.893	.004	.804	1.244
	easy access	.088	.046	.108	1.915	.056	.797	1.254
	product quality	.170	.058	.168	2.918	.004	.765	1.308
	nearby convenience stores	.034	.027	.064	1.249	.213	.968	1.033

a. Dependent variable: repurchase intention.

Figure 4.9 Multiple regression, output, III.

We observe a positive relationship between the repurchase intention and all the independent variables, that is, if they increase, the intention to repurchase will also increase. An inspection of the significance levels shows a significant relation (significance lower than 0.050) for all independent variables except easy access (v7) and nearby convenience stores (v24). This implies that easy access (v7) and nearby convenience stores (v24) should be excluded from the model; this variable does not have a significant influence on repurchase intention.

By looking at the standardized coefficients (or the *t* values), we can see that fast checkout is the most influential variable explaining repurchase intention, followed by product quality and then price. The managerial conclusion of this model is that the store manager could try to increase loyalty (repurchase intention) by improving the possibility of fast checkout, improving (perceived) product quality, and lower prices.

The diagnoses of multicollinearity indicate that there is no strong linear relationship between the independent variables, since the variance inflation factor (VIF) is lower than the threshold value of 10 Damodar (2004). Conclusion: there is no important evidence of multicollinearity.

The test to verify if the model is autoregressive was presented in Figure 4.7. The value of the Durbin–Watson statistic, equal to 1.596, must be compared to the tabulated values. As can be seen in Damodar (2004), for $k = 5$ (number of independent variables) and $n = 300$ (number of observations), the lower limit is 1.699 and the upper limit is 1.767, at the significance level of 1%. As "our" value of 1.596 is lower than the lower limit, we reject the null hypothesis, that is, the error terms are autoregressive. Thus, a correction is necessary, but we skip this step.

The normality of the error term can be seen in Figure 4.10. The P-P graph indicates a straight line, and the points are plotted next to it. In case of normality, the points tend to fall exactly above or very close to the line, as is the case here.

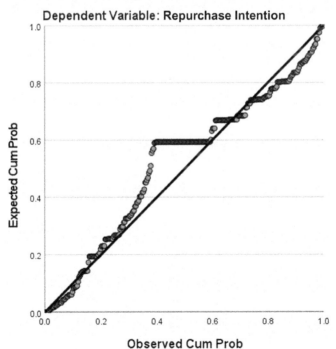

Figure 4.10 P-P plot.

ANOVA[a]

Model	Sum of Squares	df	Mean Square	F	Sig.
1 Regression	20.049	5	4.010	7.466	.000[b]
Residual	77.344	144	.537		
Total	97.393	149			

a. Dependent variable: repurchase intention.
b. Predictors: (Constant), nearby convenience stores, price, easy access, product quality, fast checkout.

Figure 4.11 Test of homoscedasticity, I.

ANOVA[a]

Model	Sum of Squares	df	Mean Square	F	Sig.
1 Regression	37.906	5	7.581	11.937	.000[b]
Residual	91.454	144	.635		
Total	129.360	149			

a. Dependent variable: repurchase intention.

Figure 4.12 Test of homoscedasticity, II.

To test homoscedasticity, we split the sample in two, each one with 150 observations. Then we ran a regression for each subsample. As shown in Figures 4.11 and 4.12, the residual mean squares are .537 and .635 respectively, and the ratio is .846. As the critical value for $F_{0.05}$ (144, 144) is 1.3166 (this number can be found in an *F*-Table), we don't reject the null hypothesis; thus, the series is homoscedastic.

Exercise

The manager of a dealership for a certain car brand suspects that its advertising expenditures are not influencing sales. They estimated a regression analysis to find out which of the following variables has the greatest influence on the dealer's vehicle sales: ad expenditures, country-wide brand sales, country-wide automotive industry sales, and interest rate. Figures 4.13 and 4.14 present the results.

1   Describe the relationship between the dependent variable with each of the independent variables. Which one is the most important?
2   Are ad expenditures relevant to increase sales?
3   What is the explanatory power of the estimated model?
4   If d_L is 1.24 and d_U is 1.73, are the residuals in this model auto-regressive?
5   Is there any problem with multicollinearity?

Model Summary[b]

Model	R	R-Squared	Adjusted R-Squared	Std. Error of the Estimate	Durbin–Watson
1	.949[a]	.901	.888	12.34502	1.498

a. Predictors: (Constant), Interest, Advertise, Industry, Brand.
b. Dependent Variable: Dealer.

Figure 4.13 Exercise, I.

Coefficients[a]

Model	Unstandardized Coefficients		Standardized Coefficients	t	Sig.	Collinearity Statistics	
	B	Std. Error	Beta			Tolerance	VIF
1 (Constant)	7.536	37.057		.203	.840		
Brand	.343	.033	1.114	10.295	.000	.273	3.663
Industry	−.002	.001	−.169	−1.710	.097	.327	3.054
Advertise	−5.612E−5	.000	−.032	−.468	.643	.676	1.478
Interest	15.558	38.513	.028	.404	.689	.684	1.463

a. Dependent variable: dealer.

Figure 4.14 Exercise, II.

Market insight

Several companies provide customer service in order to support customers before and after they purchase and use products and services. Normally, companies ask customer to evaluate the support they received, answering questions such as: what is your satisfaction with the employee who helped you today? What is your satisfaction with the solution the company offered? Was your problem totally fixed? What is your satisfaction with the support process? What is the likelihood that you will do your next purchase also at our company? How likely are you to recommend our company to friends and relatives?

Based on these questions, a regression model can be developed in order to help the company increase customer loyalty.

Suggested readings

Anderson, R. E., & Srinivasan, S. S. (2003). E-satisfaction and e-loyalty: A contingency framework. *Psychology & Marketing, 20*(2), 123–138.

Bhattacharjee, A., & Mogilner, C. (2014). Happiness from ordinary and extraordinary experiences. *Journal of Consumer Research, 41*(1), 1–17.

Caprariello, P. A., & Reis, H. T. (2013). To do, to have, or to share? Valuing experiences over material possessions depends on the involvement of others. *Journal of Personality and Social Psychology, 104*(2), 199.

Hsee, C. K., Yang, Y., Li, N., & Shen, L. (2009). Wealth, warmth, and well-being: Whether happiness is relative or absolute depends on whether it is about money, acquisition, or consumption. *Journal of Marketing Research, 46*(3), 396–409.

Jones, M. A., Mothersbaugh, D. L., & Beatty, S. E. (2000). Switching barriers and repurchase intentions in services. *Journal of Retailing, 76*(2), 259–274.

Nicolao, L., Irwin, J. R., & Goodman, J. K. (2009). Happiness for sale: Do experiential purchases make consumers happier than material purchases? *Journal of Consumer Research, 36*(2), 188–198.

Trubik, E., & Smith, M. (2000). Developing a model of customer defection in the Australian banking industry. *Managerial Auditing Journal, 15*(5), 199–208.

Wu, L. W. (2011). Satisfaction, inertia, and customer loyalty in the varying levels of the zone of tolerance and alternative attractiveness. *Journal of Services Marketing, 25*(5), 310–322.

Zeelenberg, M., & Pieters, R. (2004). Beyond valence in customer dissatisfaction: A review and new findings on behavioral responses to regret and disappointment in failed services. *Journal of Business Research, 57*(4), 445–455.

5 Time series analysis

Time series data is a series of observations on values that a variable takes at different points in time, such as hours, days, weeks, months, years, etc. There are countless examples, such as annual countries' gross nation products, monthly sales figures, number of clients attending gym classes per hour, the daily closing price of an asset at the stock market, and so on.

Time series analysis is useful to uncover patterns in the sequence of numbers, such as trends, seasonality, or other cycles, or to forecast future values. For instance, are the average sales increasing or decreasing consistently over time? In this case, a long-term trend may exist. Do the average sales of a grocery store vary systematically over the days of the week?

Some service providers present different total sales figures depending on the time or season. Hotels in touristic cities have high occupation rates in holidays and vacation periods and restaurants, hair dressers, and grocery stores have systematic daily variations over the week, while the number of public transport users presents hourly patterns. Such cases are examples of seasonality. (Inter)national economic activity often follows cyclical patterns, with consecutive years of growth followed by years of decline or even recession.

Identifying these patterns can be helpful to manage inventories, personnel, working hours, and so on. Retailers may need to anticipate orders to match their potential sales in a forthcoming season or holiday, and industries need to increase their production to meet the retailers' requirements. Likewise, service providers facing seasonal variations need to adjust their staff in order to attend the demand variation. Thus, time series analysis is a useful technique not only to uncover patterns but to predict future values, as well.

The theoretical background of time series analysis is explained in section 5.1. Section 5.2 gives examples for marketing application, and section 5.3 discusses the application of time series in IBM SPSS Statistics Software (SPSS).

5.1 Theoretical background – time series analysis

The first step is to evaluate the stability of data over time. This is referred to as data stationarity. A data series is stationary when its statistical properties such as mean and variance are constant; these statistical parameters then do not increase or decrease over time. If a time series presents trend, cycles, or seasonality, it is not stationary. To identify data stationarity, there are several statistical tests, such as the Dickey–Fuller test, the ADF test, the PP test and the KPSS stationarity test. However, in many cases, a graphical analysis, by plotting the observations over a number of months or years, might be enough. If a trend line moves upward or downward, or the variability increases or decreases, the series is not stationary.

If there is no trend in the data series, any observation Y at a time t simply reflects the random shock a at time t: $Y_t = a_t$. The random shock a has a constant mean and variance.

DOI: 10.4324/9781003196617-5

However, if there is a trend, Y also reflects the slope (θ) of the series: $Y_t = \theta_0(Y_{t-1}) + a_t$.
In this formula, the slope θ is the mean of the upward or downward trend.

After determining the existence of a pattern, we can choose the model for forecasting. Nonstationary series require smoothing methods, which work as weighted averages. The weights can be uniform, as moving averages, or follow any exponential pattern. If the series is stationary, ARIMA models are suitable.

A nonstationary series can be transformed into a stationary series by removing the trend or seasonal pattern. Trends can be removed by means of differencing (see Figures 5.1 and 5.2). This means that the value of an earlier observation is subtracted from the value of a later observation. Once the first difference is taken, another plot should be made to verify if the trend was removed (horizontal trend line). If there is still a trend in the data, a second difference has to be taken. To smooth variability, we can use logarithmic transformation.

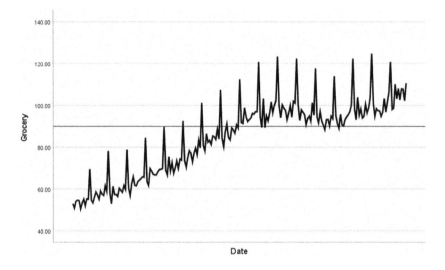

Figure 5.1 Data with a trend, before differencing.

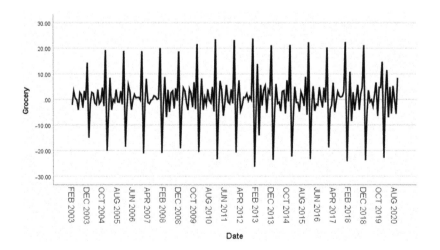

Figure 5.2 Data after taking the difference.

ARIMA (auto-regressive, integrated, and moving average) is defined by three terms: p, d, and q. The p component means the auto-regressive part, or the relationship between one observation and the preceding observation(s). In other words, it represents the lingering effect of the preceding score(s). The d element is the amount of differencing needed to remove the trend. The q component represents the relationship between an observation and preceding shock(s), which is(are) similar to random error terms. For instance, the mere possibility of a war may cause a sudden increase in the oil price, and its effect may persist for more than one period.

For example, $p = 1$ means that observation n_t is related to n_{t-1}; $d = 1$ shows that one difference was taken; and $q = 1$ means that n_t is related to s_{t-1}.

If p = 1, the model will be: $Y_t = \phi_1(Y_{t-1}) + a_t$
If q = 1, the model will be: $Y_t = a_t - \theta_1(Y_{t-1})$

To identify the number of the components p and q, we need to estimate the autocorrelation functions (ACFs) and partial autocorrelation functions (PACFs). If the ACF and PACF are significant at any lag (time periods between two observations), they should be included in the model. The plots of ACF and PACF should be compared with the idealized pattern. As general rules, according Tabachnick and Fidell (2006), a model $(p, 0, 0)$ has ACF that slowly approaches 0 and PACF that spikes at lag p. A model $(0, 0, q)$ has ACF that spikes on the first q lags and PACF that slowly declines. Figure 5.3 shows an example for p and $q = 1$.

		ACF									*PACF*							
Model	Lag	-				0				+	-				0				+
ARIMA (1, 0, 0)	1																		
	2																		
	3																		
	4																		
	5																		
	6																		
	7																		
	8																		
	9																		
	10																		
Model	Lag	-				0				+	-				0				+
ARIMA (0, 0, 1)	1																		
	2																		
	3																		
	4																		
	5																		
	6																		
	7																		
	8																		
	9																		
	10																		

Source: Tabachnick and Fidell (2006, p. 44).

Figure 5.3 ARIMA models (p and $q = 1$).

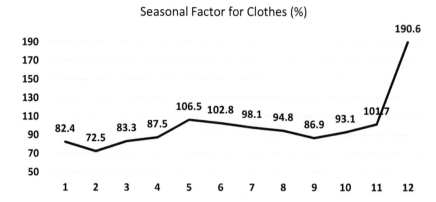

Figure 5.4 Seasonal indexes.

If the data presents seasonality, it is also possible to create seasonal indices. Seasonal indices compute the average mean per period, indicating the data pattern according to the time period. In Figure 5.4, which represents average sales per month of a fashion brand, there are two periods (seasons) of increasing sales, May and June and November and December, while there is a big decrease in January and February.

As the exact data pattern is in many cases difficult to define, we often need to perform more than one model and choose the one that presents the best fit indexes.

5.2 Marketing application of time series analysis

In some holidays, the consumption of certain products increases, such as turkey with Christmas, flowers on Valentine's Day, etc. Likewise, the ice cream consumption during summer is higher than in other seasons. Despite the certainty of the sales increase, predicting the exact sales figure is a hard task. If the product is perishable, sales lower than expected may cause losses because product had to be thrown away. Missing out on higher than expected demand obviously also leads to losses.

The prices of agricultural products normally follow a seasonal pattern. During the harvest period, the supply increases, causing price reduction. The opposite happens in off-season times, a reduction in supply followed by price increase. For both farmers and industries processing agricultural products, this variability may cause several disturbances. Even though the price variation is almost certain, the magnitudes are not, which can seriously affect profitability. Thus, forecasting future prices may enable taking preventive measures, such as investing in future markets.

Service providers frequently face variability in demand. It is a common occurrence in the hotel business, bars and restaurants, gyms, and hair dressers, among others. In all these cases the number of employees is fundamental: hiring more people than needed creates costs, hiring fewer people than needed causes loss of revenues. Therefore, a good prediction of the needed number of staff members is crucial.

In all these examples, times series analysis may be applied to forecast the future values, and reduce uncertainties.

5.3 Application of time series analysis in SPSS

Time series analysis in SPSS involves the following activities:

1   Checking the data stationarity;
2   Removing trends (by using differencing procedures);
3   Evaluation of the ARIMA model;
4   Making a forecast.

These activities are illustrated here. We use the database Sales_2015, showing the retail sales of medicines per month, from January 2015 to December 2019. Please use the following readers workshop to guide your activities.

Readers workshop

a   Open the Sales_2015 database;
b   Perform the analysis, following the steps below;
c   Define dates;
d   Check stationarity;
e   Compute the first difference, and double check stationarity;
f   Compute autocorrelations and choose the model;
g   Run the forecasting;
h   Analyze the results (power, residuals, and forecasts);

5.3.1 Data stationarity

The check of data stationarity in SPSS requires the following steps:

1   Data;
2   Define date and time;

   a   Select "Years, months";
   b   Choose start date (here – Year: 2015; Month: 1);
   c   OK;

3   Analyze;
4   Forecasting;
5   Sequence charts;

   a   Select Variable (Here: Medicine);
   b   Select Time Axis Labels (This is the time series specified by "Data – Define date and time. Here: Date. Format 'MMM YYYY'");

6   OK

Figure 5.5 Data stationarity check, I.

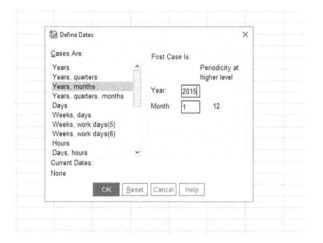

Figure 5.6 Data stationarity check, II.

Figure 5.7 Data stationarity check, III.

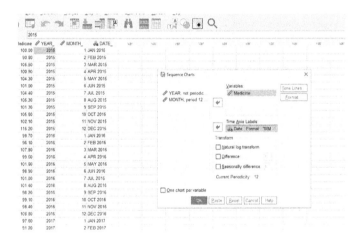

Figure 5.8 Data stationarity check, IV.

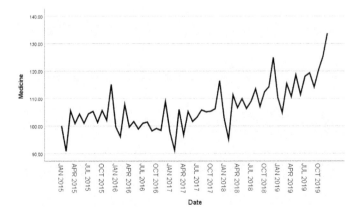

Figure 5.9 Data stationarity check, V.

The output shows a graph with the time series. Apparently, the series presents an increasing trend.

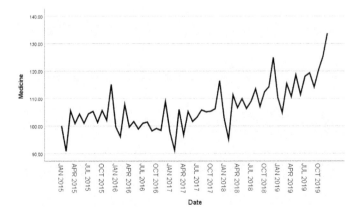

Figure 5.10 Data with trend.

5.3.2 Removing trends (by using differencing procedures)

The trend can be removed by taking the first difference. The steps are:

1   Analyze;
2   Forecasting;
3   Sequence charts;

    a   Select Difference (1);

4   OK.

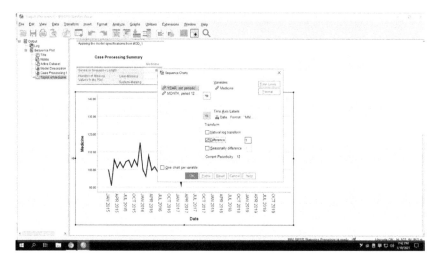

Figure 5.11 Removing trends.

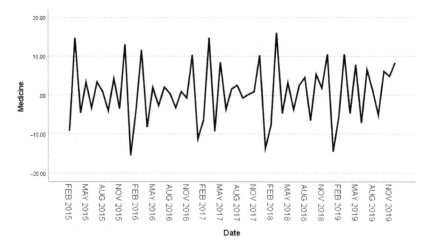

Figure 5.12 Data after removing the trend.

The output shows that the trend has now been removed, and variance is not increasing or decreasing over time. Now we can proceed to the next step, and evaluate the ARIMA model.

5.3.3 Evaluation of the ARIMA model

The ARIMA model can be evaluated by performing the following steps:

1 Analyze;
2 Forecasting;
3 Autocorrelations (keep the same variables and differences as in the previous sequence);

    a   Variables: Select Medicine;
    b   Select difference (1);

4 OK.

Figure 5.13 Evaluation ARIMA, I.

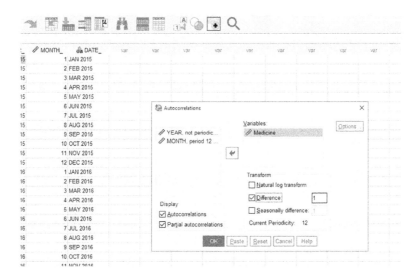

Figure 5.14 Evaluation ARIMA, II.

The output shows the following two figures.

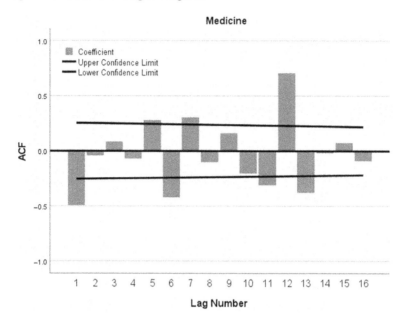

Figure 5.15 Evaluation ARIMA, III.

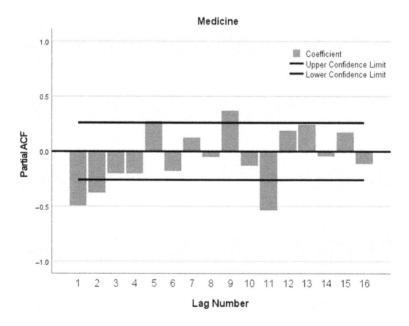

Figure 5.16 Evaluation ARIMA, IV.

As PACF slowly declines until lag 4 and ACF spikes on the first lag, we can choose the model (0, 0, 1). Considering we took the first difference, our model is ARIMA (0, 1, 1). Initially, we will perform the non-seasonal option, later the seasonal, and choose the best model.

5.3.4A Making a forecast with ARIMA

We can now forecast, by taking the following steps:

1   Analyzing;
2   Forecasting;
3   Creating traditional models;
4   Variables;

    a   Dependent Variables (Medicine);
    b   Method: ARIMA;
    c   Criteria (Nonseasonal: 0,1,1; Seasonal: 0,0,0);
    d   Continue;

5   Statistics;

    a   Choose Fit measures: Stationary R square, R square, Root mean square error, Normalized BIC;
    b   Choose Statistics for Comparing Models: Goodness of fit;
    c   Choose Statistics for Individual Models: select all;
    d   Choose Display forecasts;

6   Plots;

    a   Choose Series (default);
    b   Each Plot Displays: Observed values, Forecasts, Confidence intervals for forecasts, Confidence intervals for fit values, Residual autocorrelations (ACF) and Residual partial autocorrelations (PACF);

7   Options;

    a   Define the number of forecasts, for example 3. In this case, we move 3 months in the future by specifying "First case after end of estimation period through a specified date" as Year (2020) and Month (3);

8   OK.

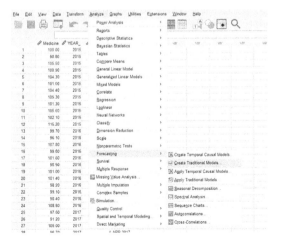

Figure 5.17 Forecast, I.

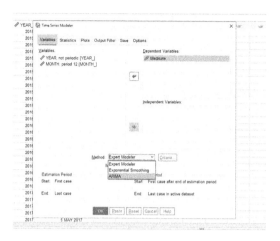

Figure 5.18 Forecast, II.

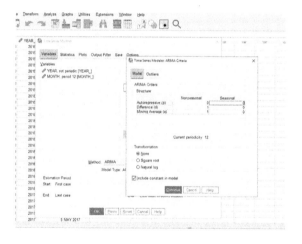

Figure 5.19 Forecast, III.

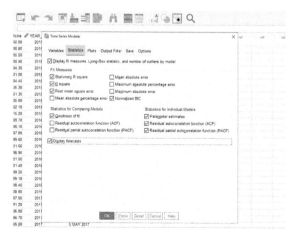

Figure 5.20 Forecast, IV.

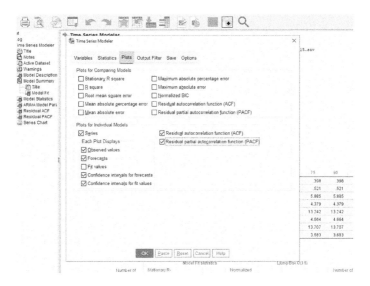

Figure 5.21 Forecast, V.

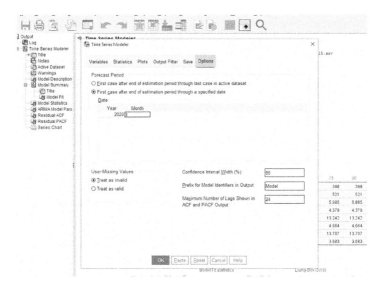

Figure 5.22 Forecast, VI.

The results show a medium explanatory power, based on *R*-squared equals 0.521; see Figure 5.23. *R*-squared can vary between 0 and 1, the latter meaning total explanation power.

The forecasted sales are: 123.4 in Jan 2020; 123.8 in Feb, and 124.21 in March. The upper and lower confidence levels are also displayed. For example, in January total sales will be between 111.78 and 135.02.

The ARIMA model parameters highlight that the first moving average is significant at .000. Apparently, there is a problem at lag 13, maybe because of seasonality. The procedure of forecasting with seasonality in SPSS is discussed in section 5.4.4B (Making a forecast with exponential smoothing).

Fit Statistic	Mean	SE	Minimum	Maximum
Stationary *R*-squared	.398	.	.398	.398
R-squared	.521	.	.521	.521
RMSE	5.885	.	5.885	5.885
MAPE	4.379	.	4.379	4.379
MaxAPE	13.242	.	13.242	13.242
MAE	4.664	.	4.664	4.664
MaxAE	13.707	.	13.707	13.707
Normalized BIC	3.683	.	3.683	3.683

Figure 5.23 Forecast, output, I.

Model		Jan 2020	Feb 2020	Mar 2020
Medicine-Model_1	Forecast	123.40	123.80	124.21
	UCL	135.02	135.70	136.38
	LCL	111.78	111.91	112.04

Note: For each model, forecasts start after the last non-missing in the range of the requested estimation period, and end at the last period for which non-missing values of all the predictors are available or at the end date of the requested forecast period, whichever is earlier.

Figure 5.24 Forecast, output, II.

		Estimate	SE	t	Sig.
Medicine- Medicine No Transformation	Constant	.405	.183	2.218	.031
Model_1	Difference	1			
	MA Lag 1	.781	.104	7.532	.000

Figure 5.25 Forecast, output, III.

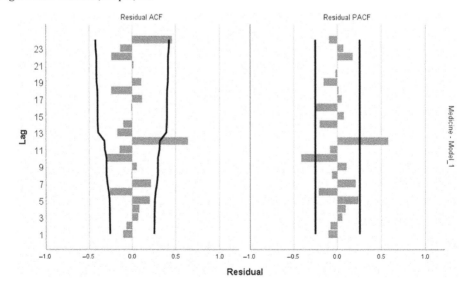

Figure 5.26 Forecast, output, IV.

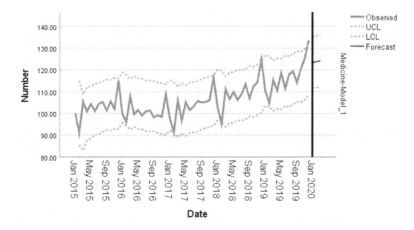

Figure 5.27 Forecast, output, V.

5.4.4B Making a forecast with exponential smoothing

If we identify any seasonality, we can choose exponential smoothing instead of an ARIMA model. This implies that we repeat the forecasting as shown before, but now with exponential smoothing.

1 Analyze;
2 Forecasting;
3 Create traditional models;
4 Variables;

   a Dependent Variables (Medicine);
   b Method: Exponential Smoothing;
   c Criteria (Winter's additive)
   d Continue;

5 Take steps 5, 6, 7, and 8, as explained under section 5.4.4A (forecast with ARIMA).

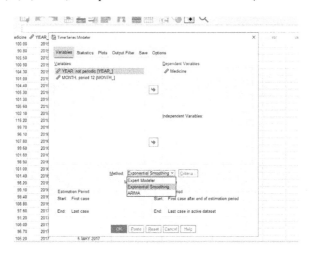

Figure 5.28 Forecast with seasonality, I.

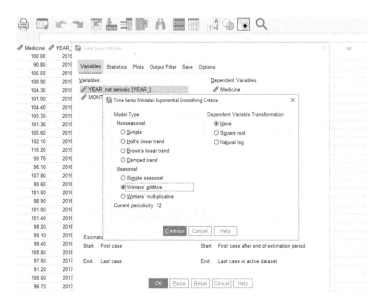

Figure 5.29 Forecast with seasonality, II.

Fit Statistic	Mean	SE	Minimum	Maximum
Stationary *R*-squared	.586	.	.586	.586
R-squared	.952	.	.952	.952
RMSE	1.867	.	1.867	1.867
MAPE	1.350	.	1.350	1.350
MaxAPE	3.860	.	3.860	3.860
MAE	1.429	.	1.429	1.429
MaxAE	4.836	.	4.836	4.836
Normalized BIC	1.453	.	1.453	1.453

Figure 5.30 Forecast with seasonality, output, I.

Model		Jan 2020	Feb 2020	Mar 2020
Medicine-Model_1	Forecast	120.32	114.36	128.48
	UCL	124.06	118.63	133.30
	LCL	116.58	110.09	123.65

Note: For each model, forecasts start after the last non-missing in the range of the requested estimation period, and end at the last period for which non-missing values of all the predictors are available or at the end date of the requested forecast period, whichever is earlier.

Figure 5.31 Forecast with seasonality, output, II.

Using exponential smoothing generates different results. The forecasted sales are smaller for Jan and Feb, and greater for Mar. As the *R*-squared is much higher (.952), this model has greater predictive power. Apparently, there is a seasonal effect. Because of the higher predictive power, exponential smoothing is preferred over ARIMA.

Exercise

A real estate company registered the monthly average rent for apartments during the years 2017–2019. Using time series analysis, the company got the following results.

1   Is the series stationary? If not, did the first difference remove the trend?
2   What model did they choose for forecasting? Is it suitable?
3   What are the forecasted values for the rent for the first half year of 2020?
4   What is the explanatory power?

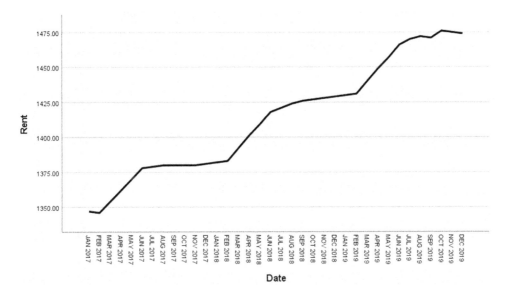

Figure 5.32 Exercise I.

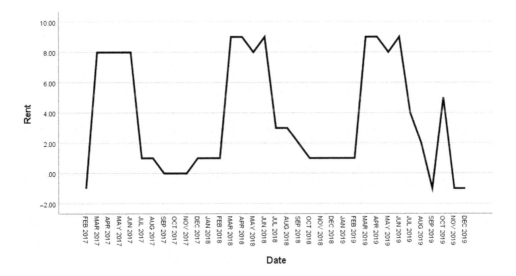

Figure 5.33 Exercise II (First difference).

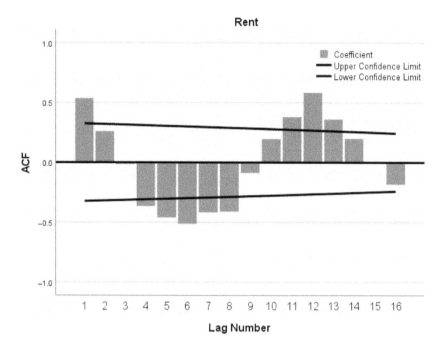

Figure 5.34 Exercise III.

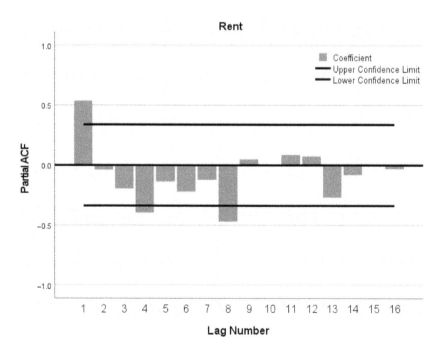

Figure 5.35 Exercise IV.

The forecasted results for Jan–Jun 2020 are shown in the following figures.

			Model Type	
Model ID	Rent	Model_1	ARIMA (1,1,0)(0,0,0)	

Figure 5.36 Exercise V.

Fit Statistic	Mean	SE	Minimum	Maximum	5	10	25	50	75	90	95
Stationary *R*-squared	.304	.	.304	.304	.304	.304	.304	.304	.304	.304	.304
R-squared	.993	.	.993	.993	.993	.993	.993	.993	.993	.993	.993
RMSE	3.216	.	3.216	3.216	3.216	3.216	3.216	3.216	3.216	3.216	3.216
MAPE	.178	.	.178	.178	.178	.178	.178	.178	.178	.178	.178
MaxAPE	.529	.	.529	.529	.529	.529	.529	.529	.529	.529	.529
MAE	2.511	.	2.511	2.511	2.511	2.511	2.511	2.511	2.511	2.511	2.511
MaxAE	7.159	.	7.159	7.159	7.159	7.159	7.159	7.159	7.159	7.159	7.159
Normalized BIC	2.539	.	2.539	2.539	2.539	2.539	2.539	2.539	2.539	2.539	2.539

Figure 5.37 Exercise VI.

Model		Jan 2020	Feb 2020	Mar 2020	Apr 2020	May 2020	Jun 2020
Rent-Model_1	Forecast	1474.84	1476.74	1479.23	1482.07	1485.11	1488.26
	UCL	1481.33	1488.82	1496.48	1503.99	1511.24	1518.20
	LCL	1468.36	1464.66	1461.98	1460.15	1458.98	1458.32

Note: For each model, forecasts start after the last non-missing in the range of the requested estimation period, and end at the last period for which non-missing values of all the predictors are available or at the end date of the requested forecast period, whichever is earlier.

Figure 5.38 Exercise VII.

Market insight

Coffee prices are highly volatile, because weather conditions in the places where coffee beans grow and the quality of the coffee bean harvest are unpredictable. Hence, coffee roasters need to carefully follow the market trends, in order to prevent supply problems. List the steps to do a time series analysis aiming at forecasting the price of coffee for the next six months.

Suggested readings

Box, G. E., Jenkins, G. M., & Reinsel, G. C. (1994). *Time series analysis: Forecasting and control.* John Wiley & Sons.

Hershberger, S. L., Molenaar, P. C., & Corneal, S. E. (1996). *A hierarchy of univariate and multivariate structural time series models. Advanced structural equation modeling: Issues and techniques* (pp. 159–194).

Tabachnick, B. G., & Fidell, L. S. (2006). *Chapter 18: Time series analysis. Using multivariate statistics* (5th ed.). Boston: Pearson International Edition. Retrieved March 16, 2021, from https://media.pearsoncmg.com/ab/ab_tabachnick_multistats_6/datafiles/M18_TABA9574_06_SE_C18.pdf

6   Discriminant analysis

In many situations, researchers need to determine the effect of independent metric variables on a nonmetric dependent variable, with two or more categories. It is not a question, as in MANOVA, of testing whether there are differences between groups but of evaluating the effects of variables in discriminating (separating) groups of a categorial variable. Thus, belonging to one group or another is defined a priori, and the purpose is to identify which independent variables are relevant in discrimination, that is, separating groups.

As an example, we can imagine which variables discriminate between buyers and non-buyers of certain products or services and likewise, which variables are responsible for repurchase/loyalty or defection of customers, for instance renewing your phone subscription at your current supplier, as opposed to switching to another supplier.

In all of these examples, the appropriate multivariate technique is discriminant analysis. When the dependent variable is divided into two categories, it is a two groups discriminant analysis and if there are more than two categories, a multiple discriminant analysis.

Section 6.1 explains the theoretical background of the discriminant analysis for two groups, section 6.2 the multiple discriminant analysis. Then a number of marketing applications are described in section 6.3, and a step-by-step description of the application of discriminant analysis in IBM SPSS Statistics Software (SPSS) is given in section 6.4. Finally, sections 6.5 and 6.6 explain logistic regression, respectively the theoretical backgrounds and the application in SPSS.

6.1 Theoretical background – two groups discriminant analysis

The process consists of estimating a linear combination that will discriminate between groups, maximizing the variance between the groups and minimizing the variance within the groups. This is achieved by estimating weights for each variable. The function is:

$$Z_{jk} = \alpha + w_1 x_{1k} + w_2 x_{2k} + \ldots + w_n x_{nk}$$

Wherein:
Z_{jk} is the discriminant Z score of the discriminant function j for object k;
α is the intercept;
W_i is the discriminant weight for the independent variable i;
X_{ik} is the independent variable i for object k.

Basically, what is sought is to estimate a function that separates the groups, as indicated in Figure 6.1.

DOI: 10.4324/9781003196617-6

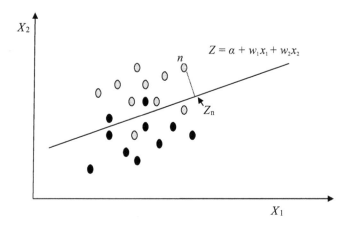

Figure 6.1 Visualization of discriminant analysis.

Computing the Z function involves the estimation of weights (w) for each variable, through the projection of the point on the Z axis. In this example, we would have the projection of the point n calculated using the formula:

$$Z_n = w_1 x_1 + w_2 x_2$$

Wherein:
$w_1 = \cos\theta$ (x_1 weight);
$w_2 = \sin\theta$ (x_2 weight);
z_n is the projection of point n on the z axis;
θ is the angle formed between the z axis and the horizontal axis x_1.

Performing the calculations for each observation, we obtain a z score for each one, which results in the estimation of a Z function. Obviously, for each different θ angle, there will be a new Z function.

For each function, the sums of squares must be calculated, that is, the total, the within groups, and the between groups sum of squares. Since the purpose of discriminant analysis is to determine a separation that maximizes the difference between groups and minimizes the difference within groups, the Z function that serves this purpose is the one that results in the largest ratio between the sum of squares between groups and the sum of squares within the group, such as:

$$\lambda = \frac{SS_{between}}{SS_{within}}$$

There is only a single angle that will maximize the ratio between the sums of squares. In summary, several Z functions are estimated through the projections of the points on the axis, and the one that provides the biggest difference between the groups and the smallest within the groups will be the chosen function.

To assess the statistical significance of the discriminant function, we must use Wilks' Lambda (Λ). However, practical significance must be assessed in another way. It is quite common to find cases in which, despite observing statistical significance, practical significance is irrelevant or nonexistent. This is often due to the sample size, as large samples allow significant statistical differences even though the differences between the groups are small.

Therefore, practical significance should be assessed. This is done by using the squared canonical correlation.

$$CR^2 = \frac{SS_{between}}{SS_{total}}$$

The squared canonical correlation indicates the proportion of the total variance that is due to the variance between groups. It can be understood as the proportion of variation in the dependent variable explained by the independent variables, that is, the variation between groups explained by the discriminating variables.

In addition to estimating a function that separates the groups and identifying the relevant variables for discrimination, the discriminant analysis also serves to classify future observations. Based on the z scores calculated for each observation, we can divide the space into collectively exhaustive and mutually exclusive parts, so that each future observation, multiplied by the discriminating scores, will be directed to one space or another. Basically, the scheme is made by calculating a cutoff value, and each observation will be included in a sub-space if it is greater or lesser than the cutoff value.

The cutoff value must be calculated in a way that minimizes classification errors, that is, it must be the one in which the smallest number of observations is included in another one to which it did not originally belong. The cost of poor classification also serves as a guide for calculating the cutoff value, that is, which type of classification error would cause the greatest damage. For example, which would be worse for a financial institution: lending money to a bad payer or denying credit to a good payer?

The assumptions that must be verified for the discriminant analysis are the same for MANOVA.

Initially, we should test the data multivariate normality, and as previously stated, due to the limited availability of direct tests, attention should be paid to univariate normality. Although the first does not guarantee the second, it at least minimizes potential problems related to the power of statistical tests. Then it is necessary to evaluate the equality of the variance and covariance matrices, which is done by the Box's M test. Also, the failure to reach this assumption can be relativized, as long as the sample is large and the groups are of equal sizes.

6.2 Theoretical background – multiple discriminant analysis

In some occasions, the dependent variable has more than two categories, for example, frequent buyers, occasional buyers, and non-buyers. Another example is the complaint behavior in the face of service failures: there are customers who do not complain, there are those who complain to providers, and there are those who complain to third parties. In such situations, the categorical variable has more than two groups, and the appropriate technique is multiple discriminant analysis.

It is in fact an extension of the two-group discriminant analysis, with the difference that more than one discriminating function will be extracted, that is, more than one Z axis will

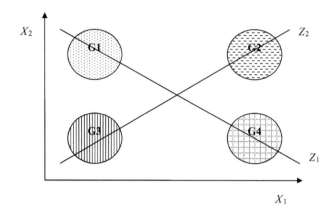

Figure 6.2 Multiple discriminant analysis.

be estimated. The number of functions can be equal to $G - 1$, with G being the number of groups (Hair et al., 2005). Therefore, we must determine how many functions will be extracted, or rather, how many discriminating functions will be necessary to enable the separation between groups.

Graphically, the situation can be seen in Figure 6.2. Consider the four distinct groups measured in variables X_1 and X_2.

According to the illustration, we can see that the Z_1 function would be efficient in separating the G2 and G3 groups, but would not be able to discriminate the rest. A second function, Z_2, could separate G1 from G4. Therefore, with multiple discriminant analysis, as many discriminating Z functions should be estimated until maximum discrimination between groups is achieved.

The estimation process is similar to the analysis of two groups; that is, through the projection of the points on the new axis, the function is calculated, so that the variance between groups is maximum and the intragroup variance is minimal. The procedures are the same as those described in the previous section.

6.3   Marketing application of discriminant analysis

More complex purchase decisions, such as a new home or a luxury car, often extend over a long period. Normally, customers look for many alternatives simultaneously, and the evaluation process requires successive contacts with vendors. If after many conversation rounds the sale does not take place, which variables caused the failure? Competitors' better offer or something inside the company? Discriminant analysis (or logistic regression, see section 6.5) is helpful in identifying these variables.

Grocery stores carry an extended product mix, with profitable and nonprofitable items. Many times, a nonprofitable product is important because it stimulates the cross-selling of a high profitable one. But whatever the reason, it is important to differentiate between profitable and nonprofitable items. What is causing this difference? Is it a low margin, a high loss due to expiration, or high storage cost?

Sales seasonality is not always related to the weather season. It may occur in shorter periods, monthly, weekly, or even daily. Seasonality of some products, such as chocolate at

Eastern, turkey at Thanksgiving, and flowers at Valentine's Day, has its clear roots. However, there are some seasonal trends with roots not easily identified. What variables cause a temporary increase or decrease of sales? Unexpected news, abrupt temperature change, holiday weeks, or wage paydays?

Service providers usually charge their customers monthly, but not every bill is paid on time; there are customers that always delay payment. What causes the difference between paying on time and paying too late? Or more specifically, which variables cause the delay? For instance, are they related to the use of the service or related to the customers' socioeconomic profile, such as income, occupation, and age?

For many services, such as phone or internet providers, banking or insurance companies, or suppliers of electricity or cable services, there is a high rate of customer defection. This is called the churn rate. Thus, it is important to measure what causes customers to walk away or to switch to the competition. Is it the service quality, the price, or a better offer from a competitor?

6.4 Application of discriminant analysis in SPSS

To illustrate discriminant analysis, we use the Gym database, about the fitness center's clients. We intend to know which variables explain the defection of customers who complained about a service failure. The variables involved are:

- severity of failure (fs1–fs5)
- complaint handling satisfaction (cs1–cs4)
- switching intention (si1–si4)
- customer defection (does the customer stay loyal or not; referred to as "follow-up" in the SPSS illustrations in Figures 6.3 through 6.6; group 1 is loyal, group 2 defects)

Discriminant analysis in SPSS requires the following steps:

1   Analyze;
2   Classify;
3   Discriminant;

    a   Select Grouping Variable (follow-up);
    b   Define Range (1–2);
    c   Select independent variables (fs1–fs5, cs1–cs4, si1–si4);

4   Select statistics, then choose Means, Univariate ANOVAs, Box's M, Fisher's;
5   Select classify, then choose: Compute from group sizes, Casewise results, Summary Table;
6   OK.

Readers workshop

a   Open the supermarket database;
b   Perform the analysis, following the steps listed;
c   Check the difference between variables means;
d   Check homoscedasticity;
e   Check the model explanatory power and significance;

f   Analyze each independent variable separately, based on relationship direction and coefficient value;
g   Check the predictive power of the model;
h   Analyze the results (what are the results' meaning?).

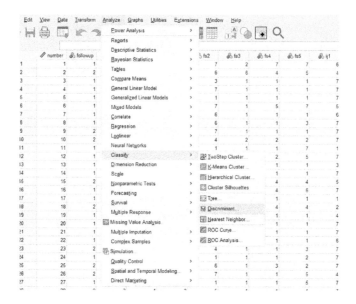

Figure 6.3 Discriminant analysis, I.

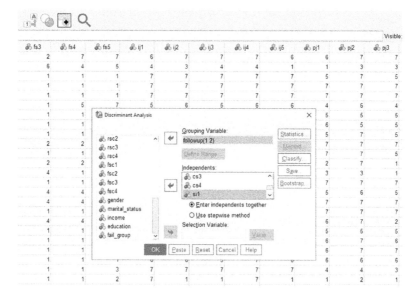

Figure 6.4 Discriminant analysis, II.

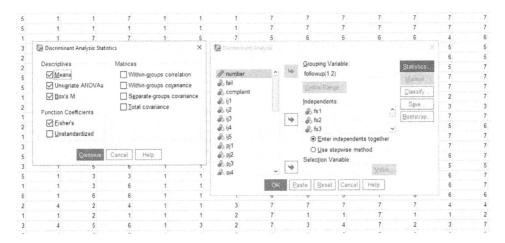

Figure 6.5 Discriminant analysis, III.

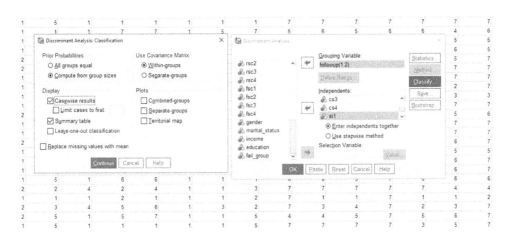

Figure 6.6 Discriminant analysis, IV.

Descriptive statistics, detailed by groups, are shown first in the output. Customers who defected, group 2, gave higher grades to all variables forming fail severity and switching intention and lower to complaint satisfaction, compared with group 1 customers. This already gives a good indication of the reasons for defection.

The univariate test for equality of means indicates that for all variables the means are statistically different, as they all have significance levels below 5%.

Follow-up		Mean	Std. Deviation	Valid N (listwise)	
				Unweighted	Weighted
permanence	fs1	3.41	2.019	181	181.000
	fs2	4.04	1.957	181	181.000
	fs3	1.81	1.452	181	181.000
	fs4	2.03	1.686	181	181.000
	fs5	2.71	2.144	181	181.000
	cs1	5.29	1.960	181	181.000
	cs2	5.04	1.906	181	181.000
	cs3	5.81	1.764	181	181.000
	cs4	5.45	1.818	181	181.000
	si1	2.23	1.892	181	181.000
	si2	2.44	2.012	181	181.000
	si3	2.46	2.064	181	181.000
	si4	2.03	1.787	181	181.000
defection	fs1	4.72	2.091	119	119.000
	fs2	5.27	1.849	119	119.000
	fs3	2.52	1.836	119	119.000
	fs4	2.82	2.280	119	119.000
	fs5	3.44	2.291	119	119.000
	cs1	4.32	2.224	119	119.000
	cs2	3.97	2.253	119	119.000
	cs3	4.76	2.181	119	119.000
	cs4	4.50	2.201	119	119.000
	si1	3.67	2.624	119	119.000
	si2	3.89	2.606	119	119.000
	si3	4.00	2.581	119	119.000
	si4	3.66	2.563	119	119.000
Total	fs1	3.93	2.143	300	300.000
	fs2	4.53	2.004	300	300.000
	fs3	2.09	1.649	300	300.000
	fs4	2.35	1.978	300	300.000
	fs5	3.00	2.228	300	300.000
	cs1	4.91	2.120	300	300.000
	cs2	4.62	2.113	300	300.000
	cs3	5.39	2.003	300	300.000
	cs4	5.07	2.029	300	300.000
	si1	2.80	2.317	300	300.000
	si2	3.02	2.371	300	300.000
	si3	3.07	2.400	300	300.000
	si4	2.67	2.269	300	300.000

Figure 6.7 Discriminant analysis, output, I.

	Wilks' Lambda	F	df1	df2	Sig.
fs1	.910	29.304	1	298	.000
fs2	.910	29.360	1	298	.000
fs3	.956	13.831	1	298	.000
fs4	.962	11.880	1	298	.001
fs5	.975	7.760	1	298	.006
cs1	.949	15.898	1	298	.000
cs2	.938	19.535	1	298	.000
cs3	.935	20.708	1	298	.000
cs4	.947	16.613	1	298	.000
si1	.907	30.470	1	298	.000
si2	.910	29.347	1	298	.000
si3	.902	32.500	1	298	.000
si4	.876	42.004	1	298	.000

Figure 6.8 Discriminant analysis, output, II.

Box's M		180.244
F	Approx.	1.885
	df1	91
	df2	202325.788
	Sig.	.000

Note: Tests null hypothesis of equal population covariance matrices.

Figure 6.9 Discriminant analysis, output, III.

Function	Eigenvalue	% of Variance	Cumulative %	Canonical Correlation
1	.214[a]	100.0	100.0	.420

a. First 1 canonical discriminant functions were used in the analysis.

Figure 6.10 Discriminant analysis, output, IV.

Test of Function(s)	Wilks' Lambda	Chi-Square	df	Sig.
1	.824	56.488	13	.000

Figure 6.11 Discriminant analysis, output, V.

For all variables, univariate normality was not achieved (not reported), nor did the M test indicate equality of the variance and covariance matrix (see Figure 6.9). However, due to sensitivity to sample size, even small differences between the covariances matrices will be statistically significant, and also considering that discriminant analysis is robust to this violation (Sharma, 1996, p. 264), we proceed with the analysis.

The discriminant function statistics are presented in Figures 6.10 and 6.11. We can observe that the canonical correlation coefficient is equal to .42 (Figure 6.10). When this outcome

	Function 1
fs1	.247
fs2	.306
fs3	.259
fs4	−.034
fs5	−.018
cs1	.234
cs2	−.314
cs3	−.071
cs4	.094
si1	−.058
si2	.022
si3	−.124
si4	.726

Figure 6.12 Discriminant analysis, output, VI.

is squared, it results in .1764, indicating that approximately 18% of the differences between the groups are explained by the independent variables. Thus, the variables forming the constructs Fail Severity, Complaint Management Handling, and Switching Intention explain 18% of customer defection.

The analysis of Wilks' Λ and its associated statistics χ^2 and F (Figure 6.11) indicate that the function is highly significant. Please note that the high level of statistical significance contrasts with the moderate explanatory power of 18% of the variables. As noted earlier, the practical significance of 18% explained variance has more relevance for the marketing professional than the theoretical significance, as expressed by Wilks' Lambda.

The discriminant weights are shown in Figure 6.12. In their standardized version, they serve to indicate the relative importance of the variables. Thus, SI_4 (0.726), CS_2 (−0.314) and FS_2 (0.306), in decreasing order, give the highest explanation of the differences between the groups.

However, this analysis can sometimes be confusing, especially when there is high collinearity between the data. In order to assess the relative importance of each variable, the analysis of the structure coefficients, or loads (Figure 6.13), must be used. These show the correlation coefficient between the discriminating score and the discriminatory variable. They vary from −1 to +1, and the closer to the absolute value of 1 the coefficient is, the higher the association between the discriminant function and the variable. By checking the coefficients, the main variable explaining the difference between the groups are SI_4, SI_3 and SI_1, and then FS_2. The sign does not affect the intensity of the relationship, only the direction; for instance, −1 means a perfect negative correlation.

Customer satisfaction handling (cs) starts to appear only in the seventh place. This is an indication that switching intention and the experienced severity of failure causes more damage than the customer satisfaction department can fix.

	Function 1
si4	.812
si3	.714
si1	.692
fs2	.679
si2	.679
fs1	.678
cs3	−.570
cs2	−.554
cs4	−.511
cs1	−.499
fs3	.466
fs4	.432
fs5	.349

Note: Pooled within-groups correlations between discriminating variables and standardized canonical discriminant functions. Variables ordered by absolute size of correlation within function.

Figure 6.13 Discriminant analysis, output, VII.

	Case number	Actual group	Predicted group	p
Original	1	1	1	.693
	2	2	1**	.388
	3	1	1	.519
	4	1	1	.828
	5	1	1	.228
	6	1	2**	.840
	7	1	1	.922
	8	1	2**	.938
	9	2	1**	.532
	10	2	2	.804

Figure 6.14 Discriminant analysis, Output, VIII.

Figure 6.14 shows the observations, their original membership group, and their classification as determined by the discriminant function. For the sake of simplicity, only part of the SPSS output was transcribed here, considering that the original table is very extensive because it presents several types of classification and their respective levels of significance. To illustrate, observation 1 originally belongs to group 1 and was classified in group 1, observation 2 belongs to group 2 but was classified in group 1, etc. This analysis is mainly relevant if the company actually knows who case number 1, 2, 3, etc., are, for instance, if the case numbers are linked to records in the customer database.

The summary table with the classification is shown in Figure 6.15. We can observe that for group 1, 151 observations were correctly classified, corresponding to a value of 83.4%, leaving 30 observations, or 16.6% of incorrect classifications. In the case of group 2, the correct classifications reach 60, or 50.4%, and the incorrect ones add up to 59, or 49.6%.

Classification Results[a]

			Predicted Group Membership		
		Follow-up	Permanence	Defection	Total
Original	Count	permanence	151	30	181
		defection	59	60	119
	%	permanence	83.4	16.6	100.0
		defection	49.6	50.4	100.0

a. 70.3% of original grouped cases correctly classified.

Figure 6.15 Discriminant analysis, output, IX.

6.5 Theoretical background – logistic regression

In many situations, logistic regression presents itself as a technique that serves as an alternative to discriminant analysis.

An important reason for using logistic regression is that it is more robust to violations of the assumption of discriminant analysis. For instance, when, among the independent variables, one or more are categorical, this violates the assumption of data having a normal distribution, since categorical data have a binomial distribution. In that case, logistic regression is the preferred method. In addition, in situations where multivariate normality or homogeneity of the variance-covariance matrix is not achieved, logistic regression may also be the most appropriate technique.

In its most usual form, the nonmetric dependent variable assumes two levels only, absence or presence of an attribute, normally labeled 0 and 1 – for instance, does the customer renew his or her internet provider subscription or not? Logistic regression seeks to determine the relevance of belonging to one group or another by calculating the probability and odds of the occurrence of this or that event. In other words, the logistic function determines the probability that an observation (for instance, customer has been complaining in the past six months about the service) belongs to a certain group (renew subscription or not).

The probability of an event (p) is calculated dividing the number of favorable occurrences (s) by the total number of occurrences (t), and the odds are calculated dividing the probability of occurrence by the probability of nonoccurrence, or:

$$p = \frac{s}{t} \quad odds = \frac{p}{1-p}$$

For example, if out of 100 customers who complained, 20 did not renew their subscriptions, the probability of nonrenewal would be 0.2 (20/100), and the odds would be ¼ {0.2/(1–0.2)}.

Next to the probability of a customer renewing his or her internet provider subscription, we can think of many other examples, such as the probability of an institution going bankrupt or not, a person suffering some type of illness or not, or a customer making a purchase or not.

Logistic regression computes the logistic function, taking into account that the values of the dependent variable must be constrained between 0 (0% probability) and 1 (100% probability). In order to compute the probability of the occurrence of an event (e.g., subscription renewal) considering only one independent variable, we use the formula:

$$p = \frac{1}{1+e^{-(\beta_0 + \beta_1 X_1)}}$$

Wherein:

p is the event occurrence probability;

e is the basis of the natural logarithm;

β_0 and β_1 are the coefficients of the logistic function.

The process of estimating parameters is the maximum likelihood estimation, and due to the lack of an analytical solution, an iterative method is usually employed (Sharma, 1996). The function can be transformed into odds ratio, which compares the probability that an event will occur with the probability that it will not. If the coefficient B_1 is positive, the probability of occurrence increases. If it is negative, the probability decreases.

$$\frac{\rho}{1-\rho} = e^{B_0 + B_1 X_1}$$

As illustrated in Figure 6.16, low values of the independent variable determine a probability that tends to 0, while high values determine a probability that tends to 1. The logistic regression curve assumes an S shape.

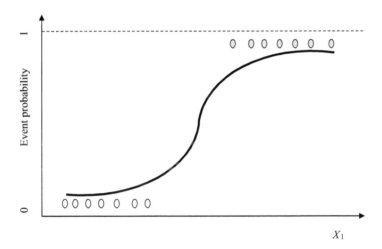

Figure 6.16 Logistic regression curve.

Once the model has been estimated, the goodness-of-fit should be assessed. The hypothesis to be tested is that the model fits the data, against the alternative that the model does not fit the data. In other words, the estimated values are not statistically different from the observed values. Therefore, the ideal is to fail the rejection of H_0: this implies that the independent variable (e.g., customer had complaints over the past six months) influences the dependent variable (probability of customer defecting).

To perform this test, the likelihood value (L) is estimated and subsequently transformed into $-2LogL$, with a minimum value equal to 0, which corresponds to a perfect fit ($-2LogL = 0$, $L = 1$). The $-2LogL$ has a χ^2 distribution, with ($n - q$) degrees of freedom, q corresponding to the number of parameters estimated in the model.

In fact, in the case of one independent variable, two $-2LogL$ statistics are provided, one for a hypothetical model containing only the intercept and another for the model including the independent variable. If there are more than one independent variable, and they are included step by step, a new $-2Log$ is calculated in each step. A low, not significant, value of $-2LogL$ confirms the relation between independent and dependent variable.

However, as there is no value available to determine a priori what the low value should be, we can assess the model fit by comparing the reduction of $-2LogL$ from one stage to the next, corresponding to test whether the coefficient β is significantly different from 0. The resulting difference must be significant to attest the importance of the independent variable(s) to explain the dependent.

Another measure to assess the model's general fit is the Hosmer–Lemeshow Test. This is a χ^2 statistic that compares the observed values with the values predicted by the estimated model. This statistic tests H_0 that there are no differences between the observed and predicted models, against the alternative that they are different. Therefore, to indicate a good fit of the logistic function – and to accept a relation between the independent variable (e.g., complaint behavior) and the dependent variable (customer defection) the ideal is not to reject H_0.

To evaluate the amount of variance accounted for by the logistic model, we can compute the pseudo R^2, or R^2 logit, according to the procedure (Hair et al., 2005):

$$R^2_{logit} = \frac{-2LogL_{null} - \left(-2LogL_{model} \right)}{-2LogL_{null}}$$

It varies between 0 and 1, the latter meaning a perfect fit (alternatively, $-2LogL = 0$). The Cox & Snell's and Nagelkerke's R^2 also serve this purpose. All three must be interpreted as if they were the coefficient of determination in linear regression, the higher the value, the greater the explained variance and the higher the fit (i.e., the better the independent variable(s) explain the dependent variable).

In addition to testing the model's general fit, we must also assess the parameters' statistical significance. The appropriate test is the Wald's statistic, which indicates whether a coefficient is significantly different from 0, a procedure similar to the t-test in linear regression. If the coefficient is significantly different from 0, the probability of the event occurring is affected by that variable.

As in the discriminant analysis, logistic regression also provides a classification matrix, indicating the group's memberships. The predictive accuracy of the model, based on the number of correct classifications, can once again be assessed.

6.6 Application of logistic regression in SPSS

To illustrate, we use the same data as used in discriminant analysis. We want to know which variables explain the defection of customers who complained about a service failure. The variables involved are:

- Severity of failure (fs1–fs5);
- Complaint handling satisfaction (cs1–cs4);
- Switching intention (si1–si4);
- Customer defection (follow-up);

The SPSS steps are:

1 Analyze;
2 Regression;
3 Binary Logistic;

   a   select dependent variable (follow-up);
   b   select covariates (fs1–fs5, cs1–cs4, si1–si4);

4 Options;

   a   Choose Classification plots;
   b   Choose Hosmer-Lemeshow goodness-of-fit;
   c   Choose Iteration history;
   d   Continue;

5 OK.

Readers workshop

a   Open the gym database;
b   Perform the analysis, following the steps listed;
c   Check the function significance;
d   Check the explanatory power;
e   Identify the significant variables;
f   Check the classification power.

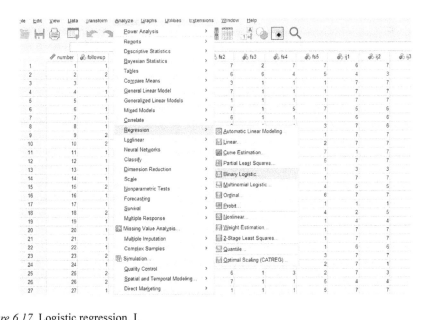

Figure 6.17 Logistic regression, I.

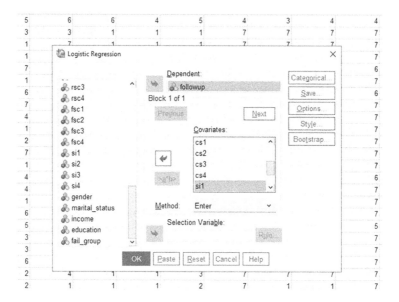

Figure 6.18 Logistic regression, II.

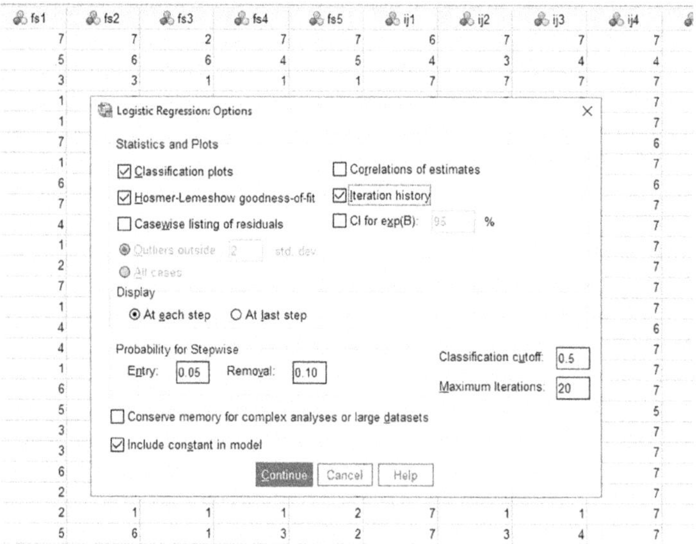

Figure 6.19 Logistic regression, III.

The results will show, initially, the −2Log*L* of the model, containing only the constant, equals 402.982 and the model itself, indicating that the constant is significant, according to the Wald test.

After showing the interaction history, omitted here, the following table indicates the significance of the new −2LogL. We observe in Figure 6.22 that its value is 347.634, showing a substantial reduction compared to the initial model (402.982). The program does not provide

Iteration History[a,b,c]

	Iteration	−2 Log likelihood	Coefficients Constant
Step 0	1	402.985	−.413
	2	402.982	−.419
	3	402.982	−.419

a. Constant is included in the model.
b. Initial −2 Log Likelihood: 402.982
c. Estimation terminated at iteration number 3 because parameter estimates changed by less than .001.

Figure 6.20 Logistic regression, output, I.

		B	S.E.	Wald	df	Sig.	Exp(B)
Step 0	Constant	−.419	.118	12.627	1	.000	.657

Figure 6.21 Logistic regression, output, II.

Step	−2 Log likelihood	Cox & Snell *R*-Squared	Nagelkerke *R*-Squared
1	347.634[a]	.168	.228

a. Estimation terminated at iteration number 4 because parameter estimates changed by less than .001.

Figure 6.22 Logistic regression, output, III.

Step	Chi-Square	df	Sig.
1	13.950	8	.083

Figure 6.23 Logistic regression, output, IV (Hosmer and Lemeshow Test).

		B	S.E.	Wald	df	Sig.	Exp(B)
Step 1[a]	fs1	.107	.084	1.626	1	.202	1.113
	fs2	.154	.088	3.075	1	.080	1.167
	fs3	.143	.101	2.003	1	.157	1.154
	fs4	−.020	.086	.054	1	.816	.980
	fs5	−.003	.070	.002	1	.965	.997
	cs1	.115	.132	.758	1	.384	1.122
	cs2	−.148	.118	1.572	1	.210	.862
	cs3	−.042	.123	.116	1	.733	.959
	cs4	.052	.132	.157	1	.692	1.054
	si1	−.027	.141	.038	1	.846	.973
	si2	.014	.123	.014	1	.906	1.015
	si3	−.054	.132	.169	1	.681	.947
	si4	.291	.154	3.578	1	.059	1.337
	Constant	−2.336	.775	9.084	1	.003	.097

a. Variable(s) entered on step 1: fs1, fs2, fs3, fs4, fs5, cs1, cs2, cs3, cs4, si1, si2, si3, si4.

Figure 6.24 Logistic regression, output, V.

Classification Table[a]

			Predicted		
			Follow-up		Percentage
Observed			Permanence	Defection	Correct
Step 1	Follow-up	permanence	152	29	84.0
		defection	58	61	51.3
	Overall Percentage				71.0

a. The cut value is .500.

Figure 6.25 Logistic regression, output, VI.

the significance level; thus, we should calculate the difference with the −Log$L$'s and its significance. The difference is 55.348. This is significant at the 0.05 level: according to a χ^2 table (which can be found online), the critical value equals 5.892, considering 13 (299–286) df). Thus, the inclusion of independent variables improves the model fit, what means that the independent variables are important to explain customer defection.

As indicated in the theoretical background, the pseudo R^2 gives a good indication of the explanatory power of the model but is not provided by SPSS. The pseudo R^2 can be calculated as:

$$R^2_{logit} = \frac{-2LogL_{null} - (-2LogL_{model})}{-2LogL_{null}} = \frac{402.982 - 347.634}{402.982} = .1374$$

Together with the R^2 of Cox and Snell (.168) and Nagelkerke (.228), this indicates a low explanatory power, or a limited practical significance.

The Homer–Lemeshow statistic (Figure 6.23) indicates that there are no differences between the observed model and the estimated model, due to the significance level of χ^2, which favors the non-rejection of H_0. Summing up, the model is significant in explaining the customer defection.

Based on the coefficients of the logistic function (Figure 6.24), we observe that only fs2 and si4 give an indication at a 10% significance level, both with a positive sign. This indicates that fs2 and si4 increase the probability of customer defection. The Exp(B) shows the change in odds, if the variable changes by one. If fs2 changes one unit, the odds of defection will increase 16.7%.

Finally, Figure 6.25 shows the number of correct answers for the estimated model. We can see that for group 0, loyal customers, there are 84% of correct cases, whereas for group 1, defection, there are 51.3% of correct answers. In general, the model was able to give a good prediction for 71% of the cases.

Exercise discriminant analysis

A car dealership is interested in assessing which variables can increase car sales. For this purpose, the company conducted a research with potential customers visiting the showroom. Later, the company split the sample in two groups, one that effectively bought the car and another that did not. Both groups replied to a survey about their satisfaction with the

Box's M		176.569
F	Approx.	2.494
	df1	66
	df2	74156.620
	Sig.	.000

Note: Tests null hypothesis of equal population covariance matrices.

Figure 6.26 Exercise discriminant analysis, I.

Function	Eigenvalue	% of Variance	Cumulative %	Canonical Correlation
1	.159a	100.0	100.0	.370

a. First 1 canonical discriminant functions were used in the analysis.

Figure 6.27 Exercise discriminant analysis, II.

Test of Function(s)	Wilks' Lambda	Chi-Square	df	Sig.
1	.863	26.058	11	.006

Figure 6.28 Exercise discriminant analysis, III.

	Function
	1
Price	.652
Used car price	.590
Souvenir/token provision	.464
Payment terms	.362
Interest rates	.322
Supplied technical assistance	.262
Serviceability during sale	.258
Required time of delivery	.250
Desired model availability	.137
Facility localization	−.101
In general terms, I was satisfied with the dealership	−.031

Note: Pooled within-groups correlations between discriminating variables and standardized canonical discriminant functions. Variables ordered by absolute size of correlation within function.

Figure 6.29 Exercise discriminant analysis, IV.

Classification Results[a]

			Predicted Group Membership		
		Type	Purchaser	Non_purchaser	Total
Original	Count	Purchaser	36	36	72
		Non_purchaser	23	89	112
	%	Purchaser	50.0	50.0	100.0
		Non_purchaser	20.5	79.5	100.0

a. 67.9% of original grouped cases correctly classified.

Figure 6.30 Exercise discriminant analysis, V.

Type		Mean	Std. Deviation	Valid *N* (listwise) Unweighted	Weighted
Purchaser	Serviceability during sale	6.8333	.55665	72	72.000
	Supplied technical assistance	6.5906	.51622	72	72.000
	Facility localization	6.3611	1.20218	72	72.000
	Desired model availability	6.3056	1.31769	72	72.000
	Required time of delivery	6.4408	1.09102	72	72.000
	Souvenir/token provision	6.0411	1.47071	72	72.000
	Price	6.4321	.72743	72	72.000
	Used car price	5.5733	1.44186	72	72.000
	Payment terms	6.5363	.61467	72	72.000
	Interest rates	5.7239	1.24840	72	72.000
	In general terms, I was satisfied with the dealership	6.6621	.76809	72	72.000
Non_ purchaser	Serviceability during sale	6.7121	.59105	112	112.000
	Supplied technical assistance	6.4711	.58650	112	112.000
	Facility localization	6.4591	1.18386	112	112.000
	Desired model availability	6.1596	1.30259	112	112.000
	Required time of delivery	6.1949	1.28054	112	112.000
	Souvenir/token provision	5.4089	1.79674	112	112.000
	Price	5.8988	1.15050	112	112.000
	Used car price	4.8246	1.63111	112	112.000
	Payment terms	6.3307	.74825	112	112.000
	Interest rates	5.3886	1.30100	112	112.000
	In general terms, I was satisfied with the dealership	6.6786	.57287	112	112.000
Total	Serviceability during sale	6.7596	.57934	184	184.000
	Supplied technical assistance	6.5178	.56165	184	184.000
	Facility localization	6.4208	1.18875	184	184.000
	Desired model availability	6.2167	1.30688	184	184.000
	Required time of delivery	6.2911	1.21282	184	184.000
	Souvenir/token provision	5.6563	1.70089	184	184.000
	Price	6.1074	1.03744	184	184.000
	Used car price	5.1176	1.59831	184	184.000
	Payment terms	6.4111	.70449	184	184.000
	Interest rates	5.5198	1.28773	184	184.000
	In general terms, I was satisfied with the dealership	6.6721	.65423	184	184.000

Figure 6.31 Exercise discriminant analysis, VI.

dealership. The questions measured the customers' satisfaction with various aspects, ranging from (1) not satisfied at all till (7) very satisfied. The results of a discriminant analysis are in the Figures 6.26 through 6.31.

1   Is the estimated function relevant in explaining whether customers purchase a car or not? What is its explanatory power?
2   Classify in descending order the five most important variables for explaining the customer's decision to buy a car.
3   Is the function effective in classifying cases into the two groups? How many cases were misclassified?
4   Based on descriptive statistics, which variable is most influential in preventing the customer from purchasing a car?

Market insight discriminant analysis

Phone companies register the client's transactions continuously. Thus, information about phone or data usage is automatically recorded, which, joined with the client's demographics or complaint behavior, can become a useful asset for management. On the other hand, phone companies register high churn rates compared to other service providers, such as fitness centers and health care providers.

Discriminant analysis can be used to prevent churn, or at least identify customers prone to defection, by looking at the client's background or usage data. Explain what such a discriminant analysis could look like.

Exercise logistic regression

A university board conducted a research to identify factors driving library usage by students. They were classified in two groups, one that went to the library (1) and another that never went to the library (0). Students answered a questionnaire with 13 attitudinal variables. A logistic regression was performed to identify which of the 13 variables are important in driving the frequency or not. The results are in Figures 6.32 through 6.37.

1   Is the model significant to explain whether students visit the library?
2   What is the explanatory power?

Iteration History[a,b,c]

Iteration		−2 Log Likelihood	Coefficients Constant
Step 0	1	325.323	.350
	2	325.323	.354
	3	325.323	.354

a. Constant is included in the model.
b. Initial −2 Log Likelihood: 325.323
c. Estimation terminated at iteration number 3 because parameter estimates changed by less than .001.

Figure 6.32 Exercise logistic regression, I.

		B	S.E.	Wald	df	Sig.	Exp(B)
Step 0	Constant	.354	.131	7.274	1	.007	1.424

Figure 6.33 Exercise logistic regression, II.

Model Summary

Step	−2 Log Likelihood	Cox & Snell R-Squared	Nagelkerke R-Squared
1	290.153[a]	.136	.184

a. Estimation terminated at iteration number 4 because parameter estimates changed by less than .001.

Figure 6.34 Exercise logistic regression, III.

Step	Chi-Square	df	Sig.
1	12.094	8	.147

Figure 6.35 Exercise logistic regression, IV.

Classification Table[a]

			Predicted		
			freq_gr		
	Observed		.00	1.00	Percentage Correct
Step 1	freq_gr	.00	53	46	53.5
		1.00	22	119	84.4
	Overall Percentage				71.7

a. The cut value is .500.

Figure 6.36 Exercise logistic regression, V.

	B	S.E.	Wald	df	Sig.	Exp(B)
1. The teachers you had in the course of your school life had the habit of attending the library.	−.079	.133	.355	1	.551	.924
2. Since you were a child you were encouraged to acquire the habit of reading.	−.016	.134	.015	1	.903	.984
3. Computers are available in the library to consult the collection database.	.317	.138	5.269	1	.022	1.373
4. Among the journals available in the library, there are titles in the area that you are most interested in.	.192	.128	2.246	1	.134	1.212
5. Whenever you needed to go to the library to do some research or reading, you found bibliographic material with the answers to your questions.	−.113	.157	.521	1	.471	.893
6. The teachers always encouraged you to go to the library in search of answers to your doubts regarding the subjects covered in the classroom.	.043	.154	.076	1	.782	1.044

Figure 6.37 Exercise logistic regression, VI.

	B	S.E.	Wald	df	Sig.	Exp(B)
7. The library's opening hours are consistent with your availability.	.149	.142	1.094	1	.296	1.160
8. The library collection has a sufficient number of titles and copies to suit all users	−.125	.126	.994	1	.319	.882
9. You have the habit of buying books and magazines.	−.191	.109	3.040	1	.081	.827
10. You know all the services the library offers.	.132	.121	1.190	1	.275	1.141
11. You have the habit of "downloading" books over the Internet.	−.100	.100	.995	1	.319	.905
12. You have the habit of reading daily.	.300	.134	5.053	1	.025	1.350
13. You, by yourself, are able to find material in the library.	.245	.122	4.030	1	.045	1.278
Constant	−2.661	.978	7.402	1	.007	.070

a. Variable(s) entered on step 1: v1, v2, v3, v4, v5, v6, v7, v8, v9, v10, v11, v12, v13.

Figure 6.37 (Continued)

3   Is the function able to classify students in students that visit the library and students that do not visit? Which group is better predicted?

4   What are the two most important variables in the model? Do they increase or decrease the probability of visiting the library?

Market insight logistic regression

Phone companies register the client's payment history. This payment history, together with information about phone or data usage, has become a useful asset for management. It is important, for instance, to identify customers who are always late in paying their bills.

How can a logistic regression be used to identify customers with a risk of delayed payment?

Suggested readings

Capraro, A. J., Broniarczyk, S., & Srivastava, R. K. (2003). Factors influencing the likelihood of customer defection: The role of consumer knowledge. *Journal of the Academy of Marketing Science, 31*(2), 164–175.

Hirschman, E. C. (1979). Differences in consumer purchase behavior by credit card payment system. *Journal of Consumer Research, 6*(1), 58–66.

Huang, M. H., & Yu, S. (1999). Are consumers inherently or situationally brand loyal? – A set inter-correlation account for conscious brand loyalty and nonconscious inertia. *Psychology & Marketing, 16*(6), 523–544.

Huang, P., Lurie, N. H., & Mitra, S. (2009). Searching for experience on the web: An empirical examination of consumer behavior for search and experience goods. *Journal of Marketing, 73*(2), 55–69.

Kim, J. C., Park, B., & Dubois, D. (2018). How consumers' political ideology and status-maintenance goals interact to shape their desire for luxury goods. *Journal of Marketing, 82*(6), 132–149.

Richins, M. L. (1997). Measuring emotions in the consumption experience. *Journal of Consumer Research, 24*(2), 127–146.

Trubik, E., & Smith, M. (2000). Developing a model of customer defection in the Australian banking industry. *Managerial Auditing Journal, 15*(5), 199–208.

7   Cluster analysis

Cluster analysis is a statistical technique used for data reduction. The purpose is to group the cases, or observations, not the variables. In a marketing context, it is a very useful technique for market segmentation.

As an example, imagine a financial institution looking to segment its customers. Based on certain financial indicators, the institution could distinguish a customer segment that would be in the market for private banking, a segment that might be interested in a new type of savings account, a segment of people that runs the risk of not repaying their debts, etc. In other words, with cluster analysis, it is possible to identify groups of customers with similar profiles according to selected segmentation variables (such as in this case of financial indicators).

Likewise, retailers seek to identify customer groups with similar behavioral profiles. By analyzing data, the retailer would be able to find segments that value low price, others that value product quality, and again others that appreciate the services offered, among others.

In both cases, cluster analysis is the most appropriate technique. Although factor analysis can also be used for segmentation, because it is based on the correlation between observations, it would not guarantee the similarity between the elements but only the analogy in behavior.

Basically, the cluster analysis seeks to identify the closest elements in the sample space and group them according to some chosen distance measure. Therefore, the elements will be grouped according to conditions a and b.

a E_i and $E_j \in C \rightarrow E_i$ and E_j are similar.
b E_i and $E_j \notin C \rightarrow E_i$ and E_j are different.

The procedure takes place as illustrated in Figure 7.1. By calculating the distance between the observations in a sample space, they are directed to the groups in a number of stages until all observations are grouped into one group.

Given the six observations in the sample space in Figure 7.1, we can group them according to the distances between them. Initially, 1 and 2 would be grouped, forming C1, then 3 and 4, forming C2, then 5 and 6, forming C3. From there, we would have to group C2 and C3, forming C4, to later group C1 and C4, then forming a single group.

Section 7.1 presents theoretical backgrounds of cluster analysis, and section 7.2 gives a couple of examples for marketing application. Sections 7.3 and 7.4 illustrate the application of cluster analysis in IBM SPSS Statistics Software (SPSS). Section 7.3 focuses on the hierarchical approach, and section 7.4 on the nonhierarchical approach.

DOI: 10.4324/9781003196617-7

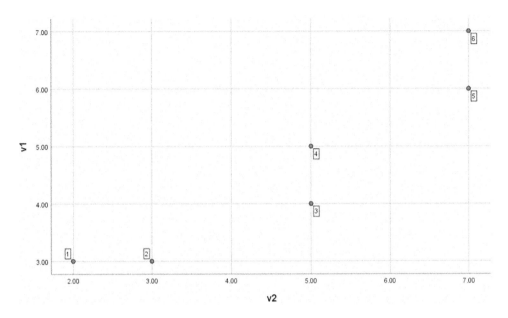

Figure 7.1 Cluster analysis.

7.1 Theoretical background – cluster analysis

Cluster analysis involves a number of steps:

1 Choice of clustering approach;
2 Choice for the measure of similarity;
3 Choice of the desired number of clusters;
4 Analysis of clustering results;
5 Validation.

7.1.1 Choice of clustering approach

There are two grouping approaches (Hair et al., 2005; Sharma, 1996):

1 Hierarchical or agglomerative. This can be done in two ways. The first starts with all the elements in one cluster, with subsequent division until a specified number of clusters is reached. The second starts with each element separately, and then the elements are grouped in successive stages, until a single group is formed that includes all the elements. In both cases, when an object is grouped, it remains there until the end.
2 Nonhierarchical. In this technique, the object can change from one cluster to another while the grouping takes place. This makes the grouping criterion better, making the results more reliable. The number of clusters is previously specified.

Hierarchical clustering approach

In the hierarchical approach, several methods can be used, such as centroid, single-linkage, average-linkage, complete-linkage, and Ward's method.

- Centroid method: the centroid is the point whose coordinates are the averages of all observations in the cluster. The grouping method is done according to the distances between its centroid, starting with those with the shortest distance. The advantage of this method is that it is the least affected by outliers.
- Simple-linkage (nearest-neighbor method): it is based on the shortest distance between two objects to form the first cluster. Then the next shortest distance is found, and either a third object is inserted into the first cluster or a second cluster is formed. Disadvantage: it generates a long chain of agglomeration and, in the end, non-similar objects can be grouped.
- Complete-linkage (farthest-neighbor method): it is similar to the simple-linkage, differing only by specifying the longest distance between objects within a cluster. Hence, all objects that have a distance between them that is smaller than this longest distance will be joined. This method eliminates the problem of forming long chains, as in the simple-linkage method.
- Average-linkage: the idea is similar to the previous ones, but it uses the average distance between objects. To eliminate the problem of extreme values, information on all objects in the cluster is used. Thus, it takes the average distance between all possible pairs.
- Ward's method: it is based on the loss of information resulting from the grouping process, measured by the total sum of squares of the deviations of each object in relation to the average of the cluster in which it was inserted. That is, it seeks to form clusters in ways that the sum of squares within groups is minimized.

The following steps illustrate the cluster process, based on centroid method, using Euclidean squared distance. Consider the observations listed in Figure 7.2, in which cases have been rated on two variables, v1 and v2.

Case number	v_1	v_2
1	3	2
2	3	3
3	5	5
4	4	5
5	6	7
6	7	7

Figure 7.2 Cluster process, centroid method, I.

By computing the distance between the elements, we obtain the following matrix (Figure 7.3). The first group to be formed could be the union of 1 and 2, or 3 and 4, or 5 and 6, as they have the smallest mutual distance. If we start with 1 and 2, then they become the first cluster (C1). The creation of C1 also changes the position of the centroid (being the average of all data points in the proximity matrix). The new proximity matrix is reproduced in Figure 7.4.

The closest observations are now 3 and 4, or 5 and 6. Creating this new group (3 and 4) makes a new proximity matrix (Figure 7.5).

Squared Euclidean Distance

Case	1	2	3	4	5	6
1	.000	1.000	10.000	13.000	34.000	41.000
2	1.000	.000	5.000	8.000	25.000	32.000
3	10.000	5.000	.000	1.000	8.000	13.000
4	13.000	8.000	1.000	.000	5.000	8.000
5	34.000	25.000	8.000	5.000	.000	1.000
6	41.000	32.000	13.000	8.000	1.000	.000

Note: This is a dissimilarity matrix.

Figure 7.3 Cluster process, centroid method, II.

Squared Euclidean Distance

Case	C1	3	4	5	6
C1	.000	7.250	10.250	29.250	36.250
3	7.250	.000	1.000	8.000	13.000
4	10.250	1.000	.000	5.000	8.000
5	29.250	8.000	5.000	.000	1.000
6	36.250	13.000	8.000	1.000	.000

Note: This is a dissimilarity matrix.

Figure 7.4 Cluster process, centroid method, III.

Squared Euclidean Distance

Case	C1	C2	5	6
C1	.000	8.500	29.250	36.250
C2	8.500	.000	6.250	10.250
5	29.250	6.250	.000	1.000
6	36.250	10.250	1.000	.000

Note: This is a dissimilarity matrix.

Figure 7.5 Cluster process, centroid method, IV.

Then we must group points 5 and 6, after which the distance matrix would be as showed in Figure 7.6.

In the next stage, we should group C2 and C3, the closest groups now, and then we can group C1.

The other methods of the hierarchical approach follow a more or less a similar procedure, with variations depending on the specific requirements of each method. These will not be elaborated here.

Nonhierarchical clustering approach

In the nonhierarchical approach, the number of clusters should be determined a priori. The process starts with the choice of one case as a cluster seed, either by the researcher or

Squared Euclidean Distance

Case	C1	C2	C3
C1	.000	8.500	32.500
C2	8.500	.000	8.000
C3	32.500	8.000	.000

Note: This is a dissimilarity matrix.

Figure 7.6 Cluster process, centroid method, V.

randomly. Three nonhierarchical methods are most frequently used, differing in some details in their agglomeration scheme:

- Sequential threshold: a central cluster is chosen, and all objects that have a distance from this central cluster that is smaller than an initially specified value are grouped together. Then a new central cluster is chosen, and the process is repeated.
- Parallel threshold: this method is similar to the previous one, but in this case, several central clusters are chosen simultaneously, and the objects located on a distance smaller than the specified value are inserted in the nearest cluster.
- Optimization: this method differs from the other two in that the objects can later be reinserted into other clusters through the optimization of criteria measures, such as the average distance to the cluster.

Both the hierarchical and the nonhierarchical approach have their advantages and disadvantages. The hierarchical method is relatively easy to read and interpret, has a logical structure, and, mainly, does not require defining the number of clusters a priori. However, it is unstable and does not allow the reallocation of one object as soon it is allocated to one cluster. Furthermore, it is heavily influenced by the first combinations (Hair et al., 2005, Sharma, 1996).

The nonhierarchical method, on the other hand, is usually more reliable and has greater flexibility during the process. However, it is necessary to define the number of clusters a priori, and it is extremely influenced by the initial seeds. Ideally, the researcher must choose the initial seeds, based on a previous hierarchical solution.

A definitive answer to the question of which method to use, hierarchical or nonhierarchical, depends on the type of problem to be studied and the type of context in which the method is applied. Consequently, it is interesting to use the two approaches in a complementary way, using the positive points of both to improve the results.

7.1.2 Choice for the measure of similarity

After choosing the clustering approach, the researcher must decide which measure of similarity to use, choosing between different types of distance measures, association measures, or correlation coefficients. The most common distance measurements are:

Minkowski Metric: $D_{ij} = \left(\sum_{k=1}^{p} (|X_{ik} - X_{jk}|)^n \right)^{1/n}$

Euclidian Distance (if $n = 2$): $D_{ij} = \left(\sum_{k=1}^{p} (X_{ik} - X_{jk})^2 \right)^{\frac{1}{2}}$

Manhattan Distance or City-Block (if $n = 1$): $D_{ij} = \left| X_{ik} - X_{jk} \right|$

Mahalanobis Distance: $MD_{ik}^2 = \dfrac{1}{1-r^2} \left[\dfrac{(x_{i1} - x_{k1})^2}{s_1^2} + \dfrac{(x_{i2} - x_{k2})^2}{s_2^2} - \dfrac{2r(x_{i1} - x_{k1})(x_{i2} - x_{k2})}{s_1 s_2} \right]$

Association coefficients are used in cases where the data correspond to binary variables. In addition to these, correlation measures such as Pearson's coefficient can also be used.

7.1.3 Choice of the desired number of clusters

Once the method and the similarity measure have been chosen, a decision has to be made about the desired number of clusters. There will always be a trade-off between the number of clusters versus homogeneity in the clusters. The smaller the number of clusters, the less homogeneous each cluster will be. However, there are no standard statistical or mathematical procedures to solve the problem. There are only guidelines. It can be based on theoretical, conceptual, or practical considerations.

Some researchers developed criteria for their research. The problem is that they are ad hoc solutions. A simple and widely used procedure is to check the similarity and distance measurements between the clusters in the agglomeration steps. A sudden increase in agglomeration coefficient may result in the formation of heterogeneous clusters. To evaluate the solution at each step taken and determine the number of clusters, the root-mean-square standard deviation (RMSSTD) can be used (Sharma, 1996, p. 198). The RMSSTD is the pooled standard deviation of all variables forming the cluster. A cluster's RMSSTD should be as small as possible. However, there is no fixed rule to say what is "small."

The R-squared (RS) measures the extent to which clusters are different from each other. Remembering that $SS_{total} = SS_{between} + SS_{within}$, the RS can be calculated as:

$$RS = \frac{SS_{between}}{SS_{total}}$$

RS ranges from 0 to 1, with 0 indicating no difference between clusters and 1 indicating maximum difference between them.

Clusters can be grouped together into a new cluster. Such a newly formed cluster is generally more heterogeneous than the previously separated clusters. The semi-partial R-squared (SPR) measures the "loss of homogeneity" due to combining clusters. SPR is defined as the difference between the pooled SS_{within} of a new cluster and the sum of the pooled SS_{within} of the clusters joined to obtain the new cluster. If the loss of homogeneity is zero, it indicates that the new cluster was obtained by joining two perfectly homogeneous clusters. If it is large, it means that by joining the two clusters, a much more heterogeneous cluster was created. For a good solution, SPR must be low.

The distance between clusters (DBC) must be small to ensure that similar groups are being clustered.

It should be noted that the distributions of all these statistics are not known, that is, they are basically heuristic.

Table 7.1 Statistics to evaluate if two clusters should be grouped together.

Statistic	Concept	Desirable Value
RMSSTD	New cluster homogeneity	Small value
SPR	Merged clusters' homogeneity	Small value
RS	Clusters' heterogeneity	High value
DBC	Merged clusters' homogeneity	Small value

Source: Sharma (1996, p. 201).

7.1.4 Analysis of clustering results

The interpretation of clusters should now lead to analysis. For this, after identifying the members of each cluster, it is possible to calculate the averages of each variable for each cluster, and based on these averages, it is possible to evaluate the characteristics of the cluster. Therefore, we try to understand what each group represents and its meaning. It is even common to name groups based on characteristics.

7.1.5 Validation

Finally, we must validate the results. A usual method is to divide the sample in two and estimate the analysis for each of the subsamples, and then check the consistency of the results.

Another possibility of validation is to compare the results to those of other similar works or to submit them to a specialist. However, due to the instability inherent in the technique, all of these procedures have a high degree of subjectivity and uncertainty.

7.2 Marketing application of cluster analysis

Segmentation is an important element in almost every marketing strategy. Even though segments are often defined based on the insights (or instincts) of the marketing or brand manager, cluster analysis is a useful tool to create a data-based segmentation.

For instance, customer complaints are relevant in many service sectors. Complaints can have different causes, and different types of complaints can also have different consequences. Using cluster analysis, a company is able to group clients by type of complaint and, perhaps more important, severity of the issue.

In the travel industry, there are many reasons to go on holiday: a relaxing break with the family, exploring new destinations, an active getaway in the mountains, adventuring in unexplored territory, etc. Cluster analysis can be helpful in segmenting the customer base of a travel agency.

A financial institution wants to segment its clients to better customize products and services. Based on customers historical data, it can find segments who are in the market for short-term loans, long-term loans, or long-term investment.

Customer preferences depend on the importance they give to product features or product benefits. In grocery stores, each customer has his/her preferences. For example, there are customers who immensely appreciate an extended product mix, others who value a low-price policy, others who prefer a polite staff, etc. In order to better design the marketing mix, managers can group customers according to their attitudes by using cluster analysis.

7.3 Application of cluster analysis in SPSS – hierarchical approach

To illustrate cluster analysis, we use the supermarket study. In order to keep the output in our description of manageable length, a reduced sample of the survey with supermarket customers is used: only the first 60 cases. In the online SPSS-files, this database is referred to as "Supermarket Reduced for Cluster Analysis." We are going to identify segments with similar behavioral characteristics in terms of the following variables:

- v_2: product variety
- v_4: fast checkout
- v_8: product quality
- v_{13}: parking lot
- v_{14}: product availability
- v_{16}: sectors' service

We will perform two analyses. In section 7.3, we use the hierarchical approach, illustrating the application of Ward's method and squared Euclidean distance. Section 7.4 focuses on the nonhierarchical approach, by giving an example of the optimizer method.

Hierarchical cluster analysis in SPSS follows a number of sequences of steps:

- Sequence 1 – choice of the number of clusters;
- Sequence 2 – allocation of cases to clusters;
- Sequence 3 – interpretation of clusters.

Sequence 1. Choice of the number of clusters

The first sequence of steps determines the number of clusters:

1 Analyze;
2 Classify;
3 Hierarchical Cluster;
4 Select variables (v2, v4, v8, v13, v14, v16);
5 Statistics:

    a   Choose Agglomeration Schedule;
    b   Continue;

6 Plots:

    a   Choose Dendrogram;
    b   Continue;

7 Method:

    a   Cluster method: Choose Ward's method;
    b   Measure: Choose Interval: Squared Euclidian Distance;
    c   Continue;

8 OK.

Readers workshop

a   Open the "Supermarket Reduced for Cluster Analysis" database;
b   Perform the analysis, following the steps listed;
c   Determine the number of clusters;
d   Run the analysis again, selecting and saving the chosen number of clusters;

e   Run the ANOVA;
f   Name the clusters;
g   Interpret the clusters.

The agglomeration schedule should be interpreted as follows: initially, cases 56 and 60 were grouped. The agglomeration coefficient indicates the distance between the formed clusters. The "Stage Cluster First Appears" column shows that two cases are being brought After

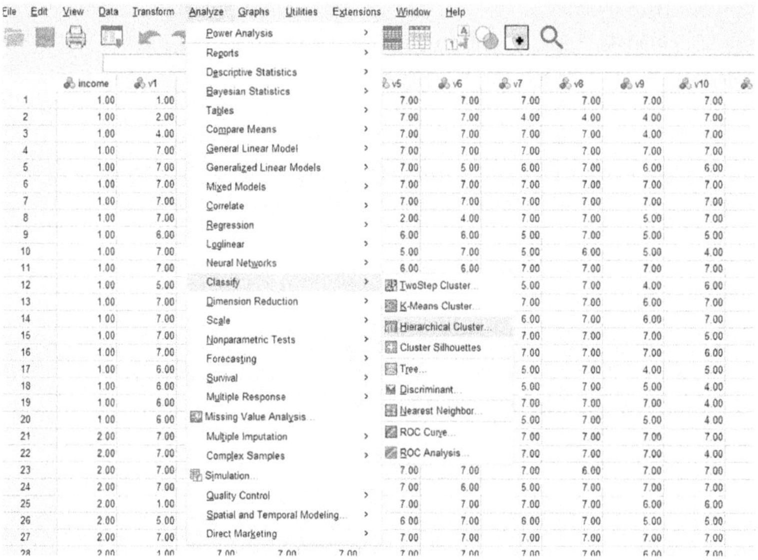

Figure 7.7 Cluster analysis, hierarchical approach – cluster creation, I.

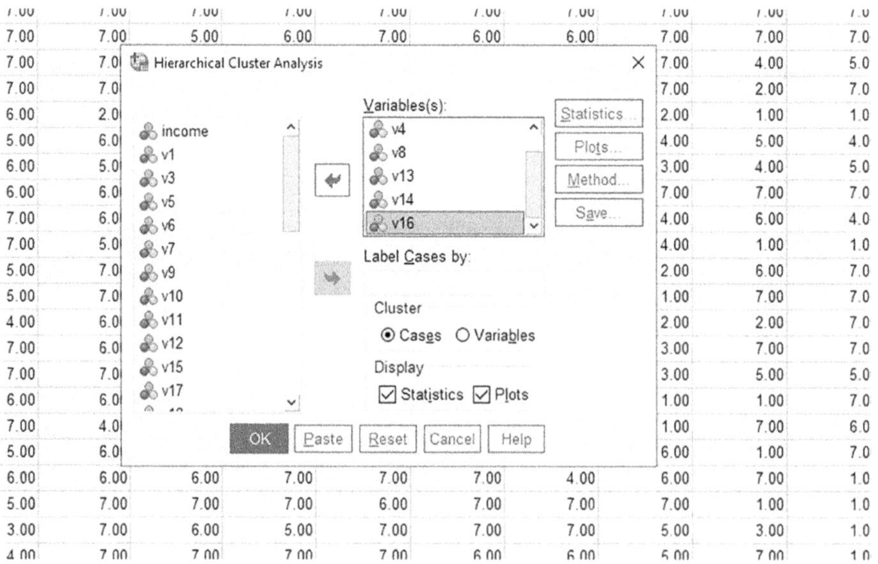

Figure 7.8 Cluster analysis, hierarchical approach – cluster creation, II.

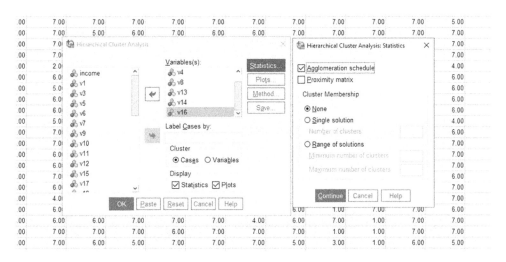

Figure 7.9 Cluster analysis, hierarchical approach – cluster creation, III.

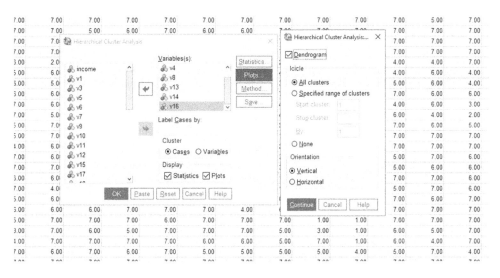

Figure 7.10 Cluster analysis, hierarchical approach – cluster creation, IV.

Figure 7.11 together when zero appears, or the number of the step in which a joining cluster was created. For instance, in stage 3, cluster 2 has the number 1, which means that this cluster was created in step 1.

In the next stage column, the number of the next stage appears in which another observation will be added to the initial two. For example, in step 3, case 55 will be combined with

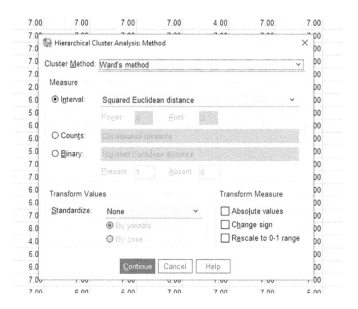

Figure 7.11 Cluster analysis, hierarchical approach – cluster creation, V.

observation 56, which had been grouped in step 1. We can see that in step 4, a new observation will be grouped.

To determine the number of groups in the final solution, we must check the increase in heterogeneity by calculating the percent change in the agglomeration coefficient (fourth column). The coefficient for 1 group solution is 986.017 and the coefficient for the solution with 2 groups is 514.616, which is equivalent to a change of 91.6% {(986.017 − 514.616)/514.616}. Thus, with the one cluster solution a heterogeneous group was formed.

Assessing the difference in the agglomeration coefficients between 2 and 3 groups, we found that the change is 35.7%, much smaller than the previous one. Between 3 and 4 groups, the change is 26.5%. So when selecting two groups, we do not join extremely different objects, as shown by the stability in the changes of agglomeration coefficients. Therefore, we choose the solution with two groups.

The so-called icicle graph and the dendrogram can also be used for the analysis. However, both suffer from the same deficiency: with a larger number of observations, their analysis becomes extremely confusing. To illustrate distance measurement, we will present a simple example, based on a reduced data set (Figure 7.13).

The icicle must be analyzed bottom-up. Based on the filled column between the cases, we can see that in step 1, observations 6 and 5 were grouped; in step 2, observations 4 and 3; in step 3, observations 2 and 1. In the fourth step, the first two groups formed were brought together.

The dendrogram (Figure 7.14) shows the observations on the vertical axis and, on the horizontal axis, the distances between the clusters. We found that initially three groups are formed, then two groups are brought together into one (5 and 6 + 3 and 4), when there is a jump on the horizontal axis (from 1 to 10, approximately). Finally, a single group is formed, with a new increase in the horizontal axis (from 8 to 25, approximately). This last stage represents the joining of very heterogeneous elements.

	Cluster Combined			Stage Cluster First Appears		
Stage	Cluster 1	Cluster 2	Coefficients	Cluster 1	Cluster 2	Next Stage
1	56	60	.000	0	0	3
2	37	57	.000	0	0	22
3	55	56	.000	0	1	4
4	53	55	.000	0	3	5
5	34	53	.000	0	4	9
6	48	52	.000	0	0	18
7	31	44	.000	0	0	25
8	22	41	.000	0	0	22
9	27	34	.000	0	5	10
10	7	27	.000	0	9	12
11	1	21	.000	0	0	19
12	5	7	.000	0	10	13
13	4	5	.000	0	12	14
14	3	4	.000	0	13	20
15	30	33	.500	0	0	29
16	17	20	1.000	0	0	39
17	11	19	1.500	0	0	26
18	6	48	2.167	0	6	40
19	1	16	2.833	11	0	44
20	3	28	3.742	14	0	27
21	38	42	4.742	0	0	36
22	22	37	5.742	8	2	29
23	25	29	6.742	0	0	38
24	12	26	7.742	0	0	37
25	24	31	9.076	0	7	31
26	11	50	10.576	17	0	30
27	3	32	12.417	20	0	40
28	46	59	14.417	0	0	43
29	22	30	16.417	22	15	51
30	11	14	18.417	26	0	44
31	23	24	20.583	0	25	38
32	43	58	23.083	0	0	46
33	13	54	25.583	0	0	54
34	15	49	28.083	0	0	45
35	9	10	30.583	0	0	37
36	38	40	33.583	21	0	42
37	9	12	36.833	35	24	47
38	23	25	40.667	31	23	51
39	17	18	44.833	16	0	49
40	3	6	49.150	27	18	50
41	8	47	54.150	0	0	43

Figure 7.12 Cluster analysis, agglomeration schedule.

	Cluster Combined			Stage Cluster First Appears		
Stage	Cluster 1	Cluster 2	Coefficients	Cluster 1	Cluster 2	Next Stage
42	38	39	59.900	36	0	46
43	8	46	66.900	41	28	55
44	1	11	74.233	19	30	50
45	2	15	81.733	0	34	49
46	38	43	89.817	42	32	53
47	9	45	99.067	37	0	54
48	35	36	111.067	0	0	56
49	2	17	124.567	45	39	52
50	1	3	139.652	44	40	52
51	22	23	156.735	29	38	58
52	1	2	173.929	50	49	59
53	38	51	197.024	46	0	55
54	9	13	222.810	47	33	57
55	8	38	250.654	43	53	56
56	8	35	299.689	55	48	57
57	8	9	379.145	56	54	58
58	8	22	514.616	57	51	59
59	1	8	986.017	52	58	0

Figure 7.12 (Continued)

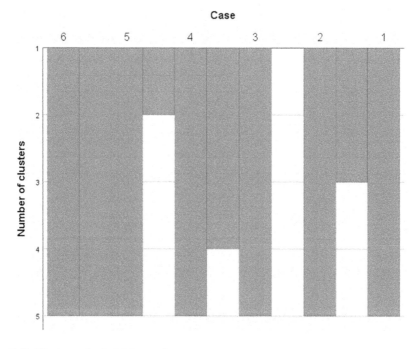

Figure 7.13 Cluster analysis, icicle graph.

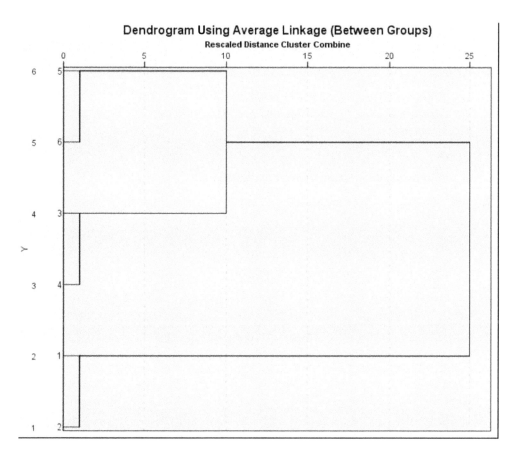

Figure 7.14 Cluster analysis, dendrogram.

Sequence 2. Allocation of cases to clusters

The next stage in the analysis is to allocate cases to the clusters. In order to do this, we need to run the analysis again in exactly the same way, but we need to add the number of clusters that we found in the previous sequence (which was two groups in our example). So, the sequence of steps is exactly the same as in the first sequence, but with the addition of step 5b and an extra step 8 to save this solution:

1   *Analyze;*
2   *Classify;*
3   *Hierarchical Cluster;*
4   *Select variables (v2, v4, v8, v13, v14, v16);*
5   *Statistics:*

    a   *Choose Agglomeration Schedule;*
    b   **Choose Single solution, number of clusters: 2;**
    c   *Continue;*

6   *Plots:*

    a   *Choose Dendrogram;*
    b   *Continue;*

7   *Method:*

    a   *Cluster method: Choose Ward's method;*
    b   *Measure: Choose Interval: Squared Euclidian Distance;*
    c   *Continue;*

8   Save:

    a   Choose Single solution, number of clusters: 2;

9   *OK.*

Figure 7.15 Cluster analysis, hierarchical approach – case allocation, I.

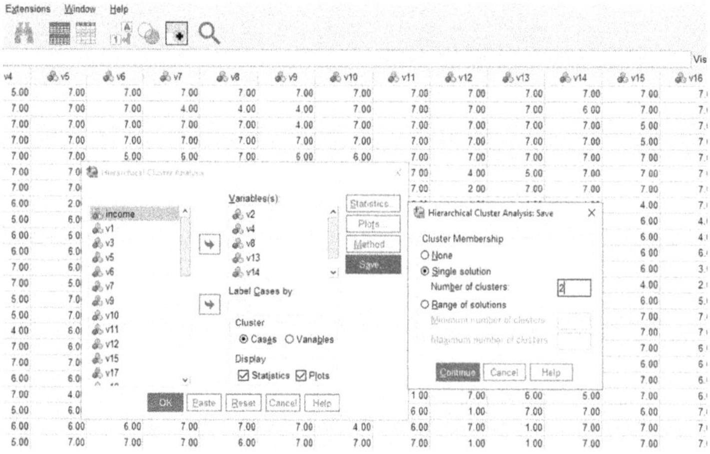

Figure 7.16 Cluster analysis, hierarchical approach – case allocation, II.

Case	Membership	Case	Membership	Case	Membership
1	1	21	1	41	2
2	1	22	2	42	2
3	1	23	2	43	2
4	1	24	2	44	2
5	1	25	2	45	2
6	1	26	2	46	2
7	1	27	1	47	2
8	2	28	1	48	1
9	2	29	2	49	1
10	2	30	2	50	1
11	1	31	2	51	2
12	2	32	1	52	1
13	2	33	2	53	1
14	1	34	1	54	2
15	1	35	2	55	1
16	1	36	2	56	1
17	1	37	2	57	2
18	1	38	2	58	2
19	1	39	2	59	2
20	1	40	2	60	1

Figure 7.17 Cluster analysis, hierarchical approach – case allocation, output.

The difference in output is an extra table, Figure 7.17, which allocates the cases to the two chosen clusters.

Sequence 3. Interpretation of clusters

We have saved the information containing the clusters' memberships, because we still have to estimate an ANOVA. The ANOVA tests whether the two groups are different from each other and helps to interpret the results. The road map is the same as described in Chapter 3:

1 *Analyze;*
2 *Compare Means;*
3 *One-Way ANOVA;*
4 *Select variable(s) for the Dependent List (v2, v4, v8, v13, v14, v16);*
5 *Select Factor (Ward Method – can be found at the bottom of the variable list);*
6 *Options: choose Descriptive and Homogeneity test of variance, then Continue;*
7 *Options: choose Post Hoc (and then select any, for instance Tukey);*
8 *OK.*

Only variables that show a significant difference between the two newly formed segments are relevant for the interpretation of segments. This can be found in the ANOVA table. Our results indicate that all means are significantly different between the two groups formed:

Now the averages of the variables in each segment (cluster) can be analyzed, with Figure 7.19. We notice that cluster 1, with 28 elements, has averages greater than 6.5 in all

		Sum of Squares	df	Mean Square	F	Sig.
v2	Between Groups	7.336	1	7.336	5.797	.019
	Within Groups	73.397	58	1.265		
	Total	80.733	59			
v4	Between Groups	21.058	1	21.058	12.739	.001
	Within Groups	95.875	58	1.653		
	Total	116.933	59			
v8	Between Groups	3.936	1	3.936	4.894	.031
	Within Groups	46.647	58	.804		
	Total	50.583	59			
v13	Between Groups	364.058	1	364.058	251.000	.000
	Within Groups	84.125	58	1.450		
	Total	448.183	59			
v14	Between Groups	47.144	1	47.144	27.456	.000
	Within Groups	99.589	58	1.717		
	Total	146.733	59			
v16	Between Groups	27.868	1	27.868	14.057	.000
	Within Groups	114.982	58	1.982		
	Total	142.850	59			

Figure 7.18 Cluster analysis, hierarchical approach – cluster interpretation, output I

		N	Mean	Std. Deviation	Std. Error	95% Confidence Interval for Mean		Minimum	Maximum
						Lower Bound	Upper Bound		
v2	1	28	6.6071	.83174	.15718	6.2846	6.9297	4.00	7.00
	2	32	*5.9063*	1.32858	.23486	5.4272	6.3853	3.00	7.00
	Total	60	6.2333	1.16977	.15102	5.9311	6.5355	3.00	7.00
v4	1	28	6.5000	.88192	.16667	6.1580	6.8420	4.00	7.00
	2	32	*5.3125*	1.55413	.27473	4.7522	5.8728	1.00	7.00
	Total	60	5.8667	1.40781	.18175	5.5030	6.2303	1.00	7.00
v8	1	28	6.8571	.59094	.11168	6.6280	7.0863	4.00	7.00
	2	32	*6.3438*	1.09572	.19370	5.9487	6.7388	3.00	7.00
	Total	60	6.5833	.92593	.11954	6.3441	6.8225	3.00	7.00
v13	1	28	6.7500	.58531	.11061	6.5230	6.9770	5.00	7.00
	2	32	*1.8125*	1.55413	.27473	1.2522	2.3728	1.00	7.00
	Total	60	4.1167	2.75614	.35582	3.4047	4.8287	1.00	7.00
v14	1	28	6.7143	.65868	.12448	6.4589	6.9697	5.00	7.00
	2	32	*4.9375*	1.68365	.29763	4.3305	5.5445	1.00	7.00
	Total	60	5.7667	1.57702	.20359	5.3593	6.1741	1.00	7.00
v16	1	28	6.6786	.61183	.11563	6.4413	6.9158	5.00	7.00
	2	32	*5.3125*	1.83931	.32515	4.6494	5.9756	2.00	7.00
	Total	60	5.9500	1.55602	.20088	5.5480	6.3520	2.00	7.00

Figure 7.19 Cluster analysis, hierarchical approach – cluster interpretation, output II.

variables, implying that for the customers of segment 1, all the attributes considered are very important.

For cluster 2, with 32 elements, however, v8, product quality, was the only variable to receive an average above 6. v13, parking lot, received a very low rating; v14, product availability, averaged below 5; and v2, product variety, v4, fast checkout and v16, special sessions service, received averages between 5 and 6;

We can conclude that customers of segment 1 are quite demanding in relation to all attributes offered by supermarkets, whereas segment 2 customers pay attention especially to product quality. This information, combined with socio-demographics about the two clusters, can be of great help to the marketing decisions of the retail store.

7.4 Application of cluster analysis in SPSS – nonhierarchical approach

In order to confirm stability of results, we also estimate a nonhierarchical analysis, by using the optimizer method and Euclidean distance. The steps are:

1 Analyze;
2 Classify;
3 K-Means Cluster;
4 Select variables (v2, v4, v8, v13, v14, v16);
5 Select number of clusters (2);
6 Save:

    a Choose cluster membership;
    b Choose distance from cluster center;
    c Continue;

7 Options:

    a Choose initial cluster center;
    b Choose ANOVA table;
    c Choose cluster information for each case;
    d Continue;

8 OK.

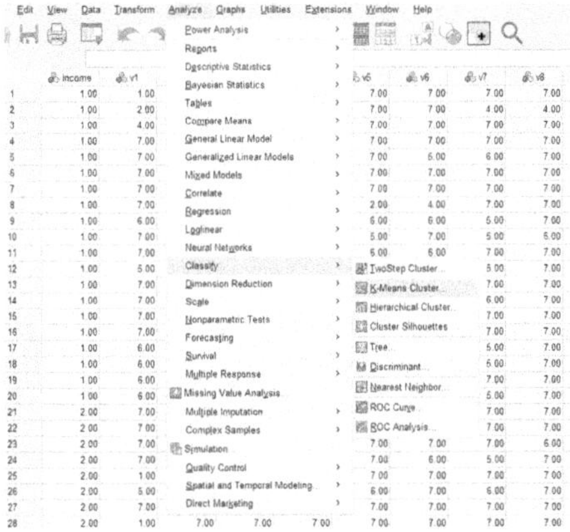

Figure 7.20 Cluster analysis, nonhierarchical approach, I.

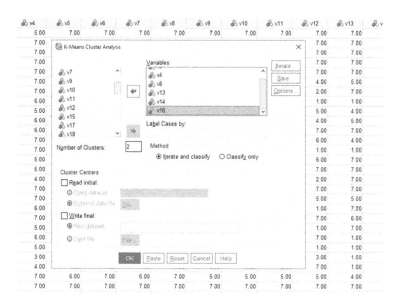

Figure 7.21 Cluster analysis, nonhierarchical approach, II.

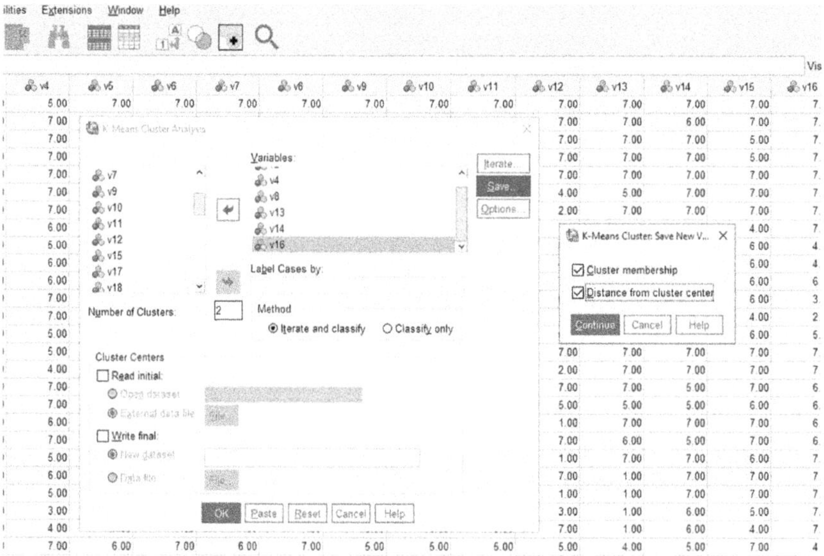

Figure 7.22 Cluster analysis, nonhierarchical approach, III.

The results will indicate the seeds chosen for the beginning of the clustering scheme; normally, you will find here the program's default.

Next the iteration history appears, and then the table with the clusters' memberships, shown in Figure 7.25. Elements 1 and 21 belong to group 1, 41 to group 2, for example.

Based on the ANOVA Table (Figure 7.26), we verified that all averages are different depending on the groupings, as indicated in the column of significance.

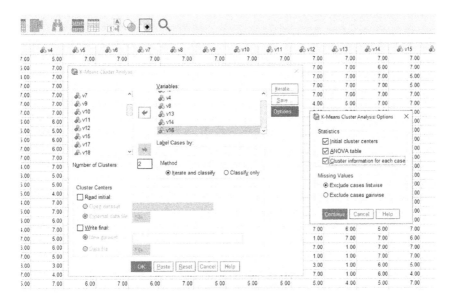

Figure 7.23 Cluster analysis, nonhierarchical approach, IV.

	Cluster	
	1	2
v2	7.00	3.00
v4	7.00	2.00
v8	7.00	3.00
v13	1.00	4.00
v14	7.00	1.00
v16	7.00	2.00

Figure 7.24 Cluster analysis, nonhierarchical approach, output I.

Case Number	Cluster	Distance	Case Number	Cluster	Distance	Case Number	Cluster	Distance
1	1	1.733	21	1	1.733	41	2	3.022
2	1	3.407	22	2	3.022	42	2	1.527
3	1	1.002	23	2	2.875	43	2	2.394
4	1	1.002	24	2	3.245	44	2	3.173
5	1	1.002	25	2	2.394	45	1	5.000
6	1	1.950	26	2	3.425	46	2	3.873
7	1	1.002	27	1	1.002	47	2	2.556
8	2	2.852	28	1	1.035	48	1	1.185
9	2	3.109	29	2	2.463	49	1	1.881

Figure 7.25 Cluster analysis, nonhierarchical approach, output II.

Case Number	Cluster	Distance	Case Number	Cluster	Distance	Case Number	Cluster	Distance
10	1	3.522	30	2	2.191	50	1	1.694
11	1	.968	31	2	3.173	51	2	5.609
12	2	4.074	32	1	1.293	52	1	1.185
13	2	4.163	33	2	2.476	53	1	1.002
14	1	2.267	34	1	1.002	54	2	4.712
15	1	3.131	35	2	7.967	55	1	1.002
16	1	2.647	36	2	4.993	56	1	1.002
17	1	1.752	37	2	3.415	57	2	3.415
18	1	2.899	38	2	.816	58	2	2.556
19	1	1.097	39	2	2.875	59	2	3.873
20	1	1.863	40	2	2.863	60	1	1.002

Figure 7.25 (Continued)

	Cluster Mean Square	df	Error Mean Square	df	F	Sig.
v2	9.600	1	1.226	58	7.828	.007
v4	24.067	1	1.601	58	15.031	.000
v8	3.750	1	.807	58	4.644	.035
v13	400.417	1	.824	58	486.200	.000
v14	35.267	1	1.922	58	18.350	.000
v16	16.017	1	2.187	58	7.324	.009

Note: The F tests should be used only for descriptive purposes, because the clusters have been chosen to maximize the differences among cases in different clusters. The observed significance levels are not corrected for this and thus cannot be interpreted as tests of the hypothesis that the cluster means are equal.

Figure 7.26 Cluster analysis, nonhierarchical approach, output III.

In Figure 7.27, we see the means for each group. For group 1, all attributes deserved ratings higher than 6, while for cluster 2, only v_8 averages higher than 6. The number of elements in each group is 30.

These results indicate a reasonable stability between the hierarchical and the nonhierarchical method, including the number of cases, and the classification of the cases to the groups (only observations 10 and 45 changed groups), in addition to the means of each group.

Exercise

A car dealership, aiming at segment its customer base, conducted a research with customers visiting the showroom. They replied to a survey about their satisfaction with the dealership. The questions measured the customers' satisfaction with various aspects of the available vehicles, ranging from (1) not satisfied at all till (7) very satisfied. A cluster analysis was performed using the variables modern design, vehicle space for passengers, vehicle luggage space, and color availability. Part of the agglomeration schedule table is showed in Figure 7.30 After Figure 7.29.

	Cluster	
	1	2
v2	6.63	5.83
v4	6.50	5.23
v8	6.83	6.33
v13	6.70	1.53
v14	6.53	5.00
v16	6.47	5.43

Figure 7.27 Cluster analysis, nonhierarchical approach, output IV.

Cluster	1	2
1		5.710
2	5.710	

Figure 7.28 Cluster analysis, nonhierarchical approach, output V.

Cluster	1	30.000
	2	30.000
Valid		60.000
Missing		.000

Figure 7.29 Cluster analysis, nonhierarchical approach, output VI.

	Cluster Combined			Stage Cluster First Appears		
Stage	Cluster 1	Cluster 2	Coefficients	Cluster 1	Cluster 2	Next Stage
1	171	184	.000	0	0	11
2	116	183	.000	0	0	130
3	162	182	.000	0	0	16
4	179	181	.000	0	0	6
5	158	180	.000	0	0	103
			. . .			
179	2	13	366.568	175	172	180
180	2	24	425.549	179	168	182
181	1	23	517.705	178	174	183
182	2	3	641.775	180	177	183
183	1	2	939.396	181	182	0

Figure 7.30 Exercise, I.

1

a   What is the first cluster formed?
b   In which stage a new element will join the first cluster?
c   How many clusters should be retained?

2   Assuming the three clusters solution, an ANOVA was performed with a Tukey HSD Post Hoc test (Figure 7.33).

a   Is there any difference between the groups? Which variable(s)?
b   Considering the multiple comparisons, which variable(s) and groups present significant difference?
c   Analyze the groups based on the descriptive statistics.

		N	Mean	Std. Deviation	Std. Error	95% Confidence Interval for Mean		Minimum	Maximum
						Lower Bound	Upper Bound		
Modern design	1	39	6.3846	.78188	.12520	6.1312	6.6381	4.00	7.00
	2	71	6.1185	1.02241	.12134	5.8765	6.3605	3.00	7.00
	3	74	6.7027	.54219	.06303	6.5771	6.8283	5.00	7.00
	Total	184	6.4098	.84369	.06220	6.2871	6.5326	3.00	7.00
Vehicle passengers' room	1	39	4.9797	1.20796	.19343	4.5882	5.3713	1.00	7.00
	2	71	6.5352	.58140	.06900	6.3976	6.6728	5.00	7.00
	3	74	6.5384	.67972	.07902	6.3809	6.6959	4.00	7.00
	Total	184	6.2068	1.01182	.07459	6.0596	6.3540	1.00	7.00
Vehicle luggage room	1	39	4.1026	1.02070	.16344	3.7717	4.4334	1.00	5.00
	2	71	6.5503	.60362	.07164	6.4074	6.6932	5.00	7.00
	3	74	6.6543	.47321	.05501	6.5447	6.7640	6.00	7.00
	Total	184	6.0733	1.22373	.09021	5.8953	6.2513	1.00	7.00
Color availability	1	39	5.1262	1.82256	.29184	4.5353	5.7170	1.00	7.00
	2	71	5.2338	1.05797	.12556	4.9834	5.4842	1.00	7.00
	3	74	6.9865	.11625	.01351	6.9596	7.0134	6.00	7.00
	Total	184	5.9159	1.37848	.10162	5.7154	6.1164	1.00	7.00

Figure 7.31 Exercise, II.

		Sum of Squares	df	Mean Square	F	Sig.
Modern design	Between Groups	12.400	2	6.200	9.521	.000
	Within Groups	117.862	181	.651		
	Total	130.262	183			
Vehicle passengers' room	Between Groups	74.515	2	37.257	59.764	.000
	Within Groups	112.837	181	.623		
	Total	187.352	183			
Vehicle luggage room	Between Groups	192.603	2	96.302	214.024	.000
	Within Groups	81.442	181	.450		
	Total	274.045	183			
Color availability	Between Groups	142.173	2	71.086	62.592	.000
	Within Groups	205.563	181	1.136		
	Total	347.736	183			

Figure 7.32 Exercise, III.

Dependent Variable	(I) Ward Method	(J) Ward Method	Mean Difference (I-J)	Std. Error	Sig.	95% Confidence Interval Lower Bound	95% Confidence Interval Upper Bound
Modern design	1	2	.26616	.16084	.226	−.1139	.6462
		3	−.31809	.15968	.117	−.6954	.0593
	2	1	−.26616	.16084	.226	−.6462	.1139
		3	−.58425*	.13406	.000	−.9010	−.2675
	3	1	.31809	.15968	.117	−.0593	.6954
		2	.58425*	.13406	.000	.2675	.9010
Vehicle passengers' room	1	2	−1.55547*	.15737	.000	−1.9274	−1.1836
		3	−1.55863*	.15624	.000	−1.9278	−1.1894
	2	1	1.55547*	.15737	.000	1.1836	1.9274
		3	−.00317	.13117	1.000	−.3131	.3068
	3	1	1.55863*	.15624	.000	1.1894	1.9278
		2	.00317	.13117	1.000	−.3068	.3131
Vehicle luggage room	1	2	−2.44772*	.13370	.000	−2.7637	−2.1318
		3	−2.55176*	.13273	.000	−2.8654	−2.2381
	2	1	2.44772*	.13370	.000	2.1318	2.7637
		3	−.10404	.11144	.620	−.3674	.1593
	3	1	2.55176*	.13273	.000	2.2381	2.8654
		2	.10404	.11144	.620	−.1593	.3674
Color availability	1	2	−.10765	.21241	.868	−.6096	.3943
		3	−1.86033*	.21087	.000	−2.3587	−1.3620
	2	1	.10765	.21241	.868	−.3943	.6096
		3	−1.75268*	.17704	.000	−2.1711	−1.3343
	3	1	1.86033*	.21087	.000	1.3620	2.3587
		2	1.75268*	.17704	.000	1.3343	2.1711

* The mean difference is significant at the 0.05 level.

Figure 7.33 Exercise, IV.

3   Finally, a crosstabulation was performed, using two demographic variables, gender and income. Analyze the clusters' profile, based on these demographics.

			Ward Method 1	Ward Method 2	Ward Method 3	Total
Gender	Female	Count	11	24	26	61
		% within Ward Method	28.2%	33.8%	35.1%	33.2%
	Male	Count	28	47	48	123
		% within Ward Method	71.8%	66.2%	64.9%	66.8%
Total		Count	39	71	74	184
		% within Ward Method	100.0%	100.0%	100.0%	100.0%

Figure 7.34 Exercise, V.

			Ward Method			
			1	2	3	Total
Income	Lower	Count	0	1	2	3
		% within Ward Method	0.0%	1.4%	2.8%	1.7%
	working	Count	5	2	8	15
		% within Ward Method	13.5%	2.9%	11.3%	8.4%
	Lower middle	Count	13	15	28	56
		% within Ward Method	35.1%	21.4%	39.4%	31.5%
	Upper middle	Count	14	32	19	65
		% within Ward Method	37.8%	45.7%	26.8%	36.5%
	Upper	Count	3	19	12	34
		% within Ward Method	8.1%	27.1%	16.9%	19.1%
	na	Count	2	1	2	5
		% within Ward Method	5.4%	1.4%	2.8%	2.8%
Total		Count	37	70	71	178
		% within Ward Method	100.0%	100.0%	100.0%	100.0%

Figure 7.35 Exercise, VI.

Market insight

In an attempt to better serve customers, many companies use a customer relationship management (CRM) system, which allows them to collect data about customers' transactions, among other functionalities. It became an important marketing tool. Retail stores, for example, can not only record the transactions history, but also have many additional possibilities to identify their customers. Several types of information can be gathered, among them: products purchased, expenses, frequency of purchase, time and date of purchase, payment method, etc.

A similar observation can be made for e-commerce websites, that can track their customers' online shopping behavior with an increasing variety of digital analytics (provided by Google Analytics or other sources).

Based on the information that a CRM system or digital analytics can provide, how can a cluster analysis be used to help customer segmentation?

Suggested readings

Bowen, J. (1990). Development of a taxonomy of services to gain strategic marketing insights. *Journal of the Academy of Marketing Science, 18*(1), 43–49.

Furse, D. H., Punj, G. N., & Stewart, D. W. (1984). A typology of individual search strategies among purchasers of new automobiles. *Journal of Consumer Research, 10*(4), 417–431.

Kim, Y. H., Lee, M. Y., & Kim, Y. K. (2011). A new shopper typology: Utilitarian and hedonic perspectives. *Journal of Global Academy of Marketing, 21*(2), 102–113.

Papadopoulos, N., Martín, O. M., Cleveland, M., & Laroche, M. (2011). Identity, demographics, and consumer behaviors. *International Marketing Review, 28*(3), 244–266.

Singh, J. (1990). A typology of consumer dissatisfaction response styles. *Journal of Retailing, 66*(1), 57.

Zampetakis, L. A. (2014). The emotional dimension of the consumption of luxury counterfeit goods: An empirical taxonomy. *Marketing Intelligence & Planning, 32*(1), 21–40.

8 Exploratory Factor Analysis (EFA)

Some variables cannot be directly observed, but they depend on other variables to be measured. They are called latent variables, or constructs. Let's imagine the concept of brand loyalty. How many dimensions would be necessary for its precise definition? Would it be the favorable attitude, a consistent pattern of repurchase, or both? And which variables determine attitude and repurchase?

A survey to assess customer loyalty could not be carried out based on a single question (What is your loyalty to brand X, for example), as it would represent a poor measure of the customer's evaluation of his or her loyalty, since each customer would have their own way to assess how loyal they are to that brand. Such a survey would not be able to identify if the customers want to repurchase, if they actually repurchase, if they will recommend the brand, if they will remain loyal if a competitor offers a similar product, among many other dimensions. It is not difficult to see that an assessment made under these conditions would be practically useless, as it would not be able to capture the customers' feelings. What is actually needed is an assessment of the dimensions (factors) underlying customer loyalty. And to do this, factor analysis can be used.

In addition to loyalty, many other examples can be listed: satisfaction, perceived value, service quality, store image, commitment, inertia, and switching intention, among many others. Most marketing concepts have underlying dimensions that need to be investigated before marketing advice can be given or a marketing strategy can be recommended.

Section 8.1 explains the theoretical background of the (exploratory) factor analysis. Then a number of marketing applications are described in section 8.2, and a step-by-step description of the application of (exploratory) factor analysis in IBM SPSS Statistics Software (SPSS) is given in section 8.3.

8.1 Theoretical background – exploratory factor analysis

Factor analysis is a multivariate statistical technique that serves to estimate a measure of these underlying dimensions, as it identifies the relationships between a set of observable variables, also called indicators, and a latent variable. This latent factor is the dimension we wish to investigate; it is called a factor or a construct in factor analysis. Examples of factors in a marketing context are for instance attitudinal loyalty and behavioral loyalty (as underlying factors for brand loyalty) or usage satisfaction and brand personality as examples of underlying factors for brand image, and many more.

Another possible application of factor analysis is to summarize the available data. In some situations, the number of variables under analysis is so numerous that the results are confusing

DOI: 10.4324/9781003196617-8

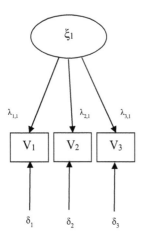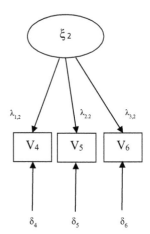

Figure 8.1 Illustration of exploratory factor analysis.

and useless. In this sense, factor analysis lends itself to reducing the number of observable variables; that is, it manages to reduce them to an adequate number of constructs/factors.

There are two types of factor analysis: the first is called exploratory, because it allows variables to be grouped into constructs based on the correlations between them; the second, called confirmatory, is estimated with a priori determination of which variables will compose each factor. Confirmatory Factor Analysis is discussed in the next chapter; in this chapter we focus on exploratory factor analysis. The idea behind exploratory factor analysis is depicted in Figure 8.1.

ξ_1 and ξ_2 represent the latent construct (we use the terms factor and construct interchangeably), v_1–v_6 are the measured variables (indicators), $\lambda_{1,1}$–$\lambda_{3,2}$ are the factor loadings, which measure the relationship between the latent construct and its indicators, and δ_1–δ_6 represent the error, or the indicators' variance not explained by the latent construct. For example, the construct ξ_1 could represent the construct brand engagement, and brand engagement could be represented by three variables (indicators):

- v_1: the intention to repurchase the brand;
- v_2: the intention to recommend the brand to family and friends;
- v_3: the number of "likes" that the individual gave to the brand on social media.

The most common methods to compute the exploratory factor analysis are principal component analysis and principal axis analysis (Hair et al., 2005; Sharma, 1996), both available in SPSS. In the principal component analysis, the steps to compute the factor loadings are as follows:

1   New axes (dimensions) are estimated for several possible angles, through the projection of the points (considering only two variables, the formula is: $\cos\theta \times X_1 + \sin\theta \times X_2$);
2   The variance of each new dimension (axis) is estimated;
3   The solution chosen will be the one that shares the greatest variance with the data; that is, it is now a question of finding the dimension that shares the greatest proportion of variance in relation to the total variance of the data set.

The variance of each variable (indicator) can be decomposed into two parts: one that is shared with each factor, called common variance, and another that is not shared with the estimated factors, called specific or unique variance. Since the factor loading represents the correlation between an indicator and a factor, the common variance between an indicator and the factor is represented by the squared factor loadings. The sum of the variances shared with the various factors is called total commonality. Therefore, the specific or unique variance will be given by the subtraction 1 − commonality.

Some decisions must be made when computing an exploratory factor analysis. Initially, how many factors should be retained? The factorial solution will estimate as many factors as there are variables, so the researcher will need to define a criterion to make this decision. To answer this question, several methods can be used.

The most common criterion is to retain only those factors that have eigenvalues, or latent roots, greater than 1. This judgment is based on the fact that each variable individually contributes a value equal to 1 of the total eigenvalue. If the factor does not have a latent root equal to or greater than 1, there is no point in retaining it, as it explains less than one variable individually. Another alternative requires the elaboration of a graph, called a scree plot, in which the eigenvalue will be plotted on the vertical axis and the number of factors on the horizontal axis. The point at which the resulting curve makes an elbow determines the number of factors to be extracted. That is, from that point on, the single variance starts to be superior to the common variance.

It is also possible, and sometimes common, to define the number of factors a priori. Such a solution is based on theoretical models already tested, for which a confirmation or a simple reapplication is sought. Thus, what determines the number of factors becomes the theoretical models that support the research. Another criterion is based on the explained variance, according to which the number of factors retained must be the one that provides a determined value of explained variance, 50%, 60%, depending on the research purposes.

In addition to the number of factors, the method for estimation must also be defined. Among the most used techniques, the principal component analysis and principal axis analysis stand out. In the first, we seek to achieve the solution in which the smallest number of factors is responsible for the largest portion of the variance. When the objective is to find the constructs represented in the original variables, the second is the most appropriate.

Determining the criteria for the inclusion of variables in the factorial solution also deserves special attention. At first, a variable could only compose the results if it presents a minimum common variance or its equivalent factor loading. There is no statistically defined value for this, but some authors, including Hair et al. (2005), suggest as acceptable a minimum factor loading equal to ±0.30, but to achieve practical significance, a loading of at least ±0.50 would be necessary. Another important aspect concerns the total commonality of the indicators, which indicates the variance of the indicator shared with the factorial solution (sum of common variances). The minimum value for this parameter is 0.5, according to the same authors.

Subsequently, attention should be paid to the need for factor rotation. This adjustment basically serves to provide easier interpretation of the solution reached. The explanation is based on the fact that the first factor is estimated by seeking to obtain the highest proportion of shared variance, the second factor will be responsible for the second highest proportion, and so on. The factors will be orthogonal to each other, and the matrix of factorial loadings will be somewhat confusing in terms of interpretation. The rotation will serve to better distribute the indicators, facilitating the factors' interpretation, as illustrated in Figure 8.2. The observations are well distributed in relation to the non-rotated axes; however, they are very close to the rotated axes. In this way, the factors' interpretation is simpler.

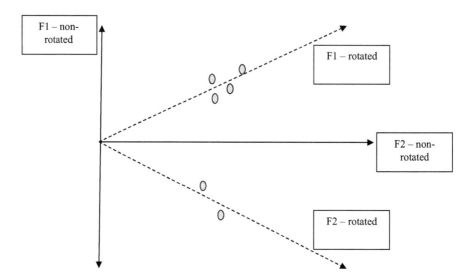

Figure 8.2 Factor rotation.

Several rotation methods are available in statistical software, some orthogonal and others oblique. Among the orthogonal, the Varimax rotation seeks to simplify the columns of the matrix, that is, each variable must have a high loading on a single factor and low loadings on the others. In Quartimax rotation, we seek to place many variables with high loadings in a single factor. This solution should only be adopted when it is assumed that there is a general factor underlying the data set. Oblique rotations are characterized by the correlation between the factors but basically meet the same objectives as orthogonal rotations. The most common are: Oblimin, Promax, Orthoblique, and Doblimin. The choice between one method and the other cannot be made based on statistical criteria, but it must follow the specific needs of the research problem.

After finding the solution, the factors must be named by the researcher himself. There are no specific rules for this task, but one should look for a concept that is well applicable to the set of indicators that make up the construct, especially those that have the highest loadings.

As the factorial solution is free, that is, the variables are grouped according to their correlations with the factor, it is essential to evaluate the validity, reliability, and dimensionality of the scale. *Reliability* measures the consistency between the variables that make up the factor. A widely used test for this purpose is the Cronbach's alpha coefficient, which should have a minimum value of 0.7. However, an alpha of 0.6 is acceptable for exploratory studies.

Validity must be assessed in three aspects: convergent, discriminant, and face validity. Convergent validity seeks to determine whether two different measures of the same concept are correlated. Discriminant validity assesses the correlation (or the absence of correlation) between different constructs: the idea is that different constructs should have a relatively low correlation. Content or face validity is a qualitative judgment whether the conceptual definition of a construct is adequately related to the indicators that compose it.

Dimensionality is related to the number of concepts, or dimensions, underlying a factor. Unidimensionality means that each factor refers only to a concept, or to a single dimension.

It is also important to measure the generalization of the results, that is, if they can be generalized to the entire population, or if they are specific to the sample under observation. For that, we can reapply the test in another sample or divide the sample in two separate samples and check the stability of the results. Dividing the sample in half is possible as long as the number of observations allows it. An alternative is to perform a confirmatory factor analysis. This technique is explained in the next chapter.

It is also worth highlighting the assumptions required for factor analysis. The assumptions of normality, homoscedasticity, and linearity are more conceptual than, properly speaking, a statistical requirement (Hair et al., 2005). However, it should be assessed whether the data matrix has significant correlations that are sufficient to estimate a factor analysis. For this purpose, Bartlett's sphericity test is widely used. This test assesses whether, in a correlation matrix, there are significant correlations between the variables. The Kaiser–Meyer–Olkin sample adequacy measure (MSA) can also be used. According to this test, if a variable is perfectly predicted by other variables, the coefficient will be equal to one. For the MSA, a value equal to or greater than 0.5 is considered acceptable.

Finally, it should be noted that the number of observations must be five times greater than the number of variables, the ideal being ten, and that there must be at least two variables for each construct.

8.2 Marketing application of exploratory factor analysis

Service quality is a well-studied topic, with many scales already being validated, for example, ServQual and ServPerf. Both scales have the same five dimensions: reliability, responsiveness, assurance, empathy, and tangibility. However, they are generic scales that do not measure specific aspects of services. Thus, there are still gaps to be filled. For example, what are the main quality dimensions of restaurants, barbershop, beauty salon, fitness center, phone companies, bank, etc.? Exploratory Factor Analysis (EFA) becomes a helpful tool to identify the most valuable dimensions for each of these service categories.

Preferences for creative performances or entertainment vary from person to person. What makes a person prefer classical music or clubbing events? The same question applies to film genre, concerts, plays, painting, and so on. Is it a family heritage, influence of friends, life cycle, or inner characteristic? EFA might be able to answer this question.

Social sciences in general deal with latent variables, which are variables that cannot be measured by a single indicator, as they are multifaceted. Loyalty, satisfaction, commitment, brand or store image, and performance are all examples of latent variables. Identifying the dimensions that form these latent variables in a specific context is another possible application of EFA.

Emotions and moods are common responses consumers have when exposed to many situations. The purchase of a good, desired for a long time, will cause several positive emotions. Identifying these underlying emotions is important to marketing managers to better develop products and related advertising. Likewise, what are the emotional responses arising from threats due to climate change, economic crises, or pandemics?

The choice for a specific company, let's say a grocery store, has several attributes, many times forming an endless list. So management should know how these attributes can be grouped, related to higher dimensions, such as product, personnel, location, online presence, price policy, and infrastructure, etc. Moreover, it's important to measure which dimensions have the biggest influence in driving customers' preference.

8.3 Application of exploratory factor analysis in SPSS

As an illustration, we develop an exploratory factor analysis to reduce the attributes responsible for the choice of a specific supermarket store to a smaller number of dimensions.

The initial database is composed of 35 variables, but for our purpose, we will explore only the following 7 variables:

v_2: product variety;
v_8: product quality;
v_{14}: product availability;
v_{29}: complaints handling;
v_{30}: perishable products' quality;
v_{31}: opening hours;
v_{32}: lowest price guarantee.

An exploratory factor analysis in SPSS involves the following steps:

1   Analyze;
2   Dimension Reduction;
3   Factor;
4   Select variables (v2, v8, v14, v29, v30, v31, v32);
5   Descriptives:

   a   Choose Initial solution;
   b   Choose KMO and Bartlett's test of sphericity;
   c   Continue;

6   Extraction:

   a   Choose Principal components (this is the default);
   b   Choose Scree plot;
   c   Continue;

7   Rotation:

   a   Choose Method Varimax;
   b   Choose Display: Rotated solution, Loading plot(s);
   c   Continue;

8   Options:

   a   Choose Sorted by size;
   b   Choose Suppress small coefficients; absolute values less than (.4 or .3);
   c   Continue;

9   OK.

Readers workshop

a   Open the supermarket database;
b   Perform the analysis, following the steps above;
c   Check the sample adequacy;

d   Determine the number of factors;
e   Check the communalities;
f   Check the rotated factor solution;
g   Name the factors;
h   Check reliability (perform reliability analysis);
i   Check validity (convergent, discriminant, and face): perform a new factor analysis, saving the factor scores; create summated scales, calculate correlation);
j   Check unidimensionality (perform factor analysis for each factor individually).

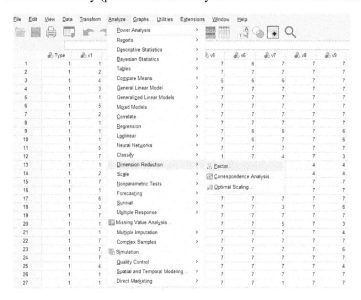

Figure 8.3 Exploratory factor analysis, I.

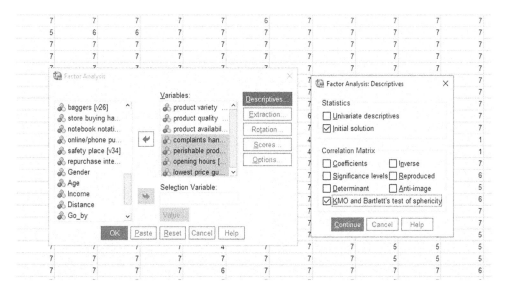

Figure 8.4 Exploratory factor analysis, II.

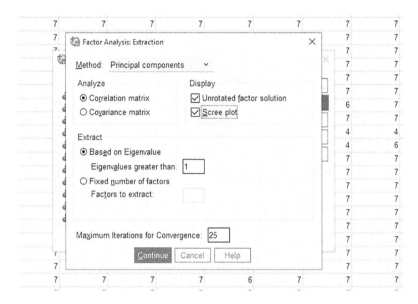

Figure 8.5 Exploratory factor analysis, III.

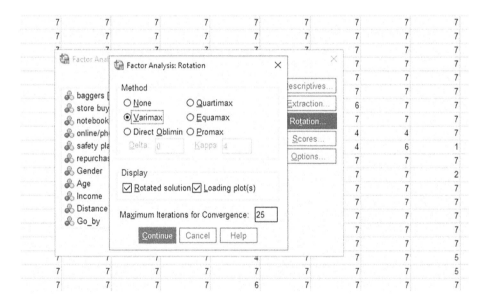

Figure 8.6 Exploratory factor analysis, IV.

Initially, we must analyze if the assumptions were accomplished. We can see that there are enough correlations to perform the factor analysis, since the Bartlett Test indicates the rejection of the H_0 of no statistically significant correlations between the variables, and the Measure of Sampling Adequacy is .686, above the minimum value indicated.

Next, we must assess the number of retained factors. From Figure 8.9, we observed that only two factors have eigenvalues greater than one, which explain 58.828% of the data

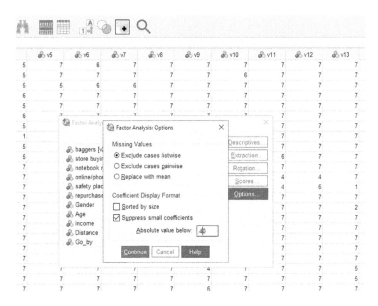

Figure 8.7 Exploratory factor analysis, V.

Kaiser-Meyer-Olkin Measure of Sampling Adequacy		.686
Bartlett's Test of Sphericity	Approx. Chi-Square	430.258
	df	21
	Sig.	.000

Figure 8.8 Exploratory factor analysis, output I.

	Initial Eigenvalues			Extraction Sums of Squared Loadings			Rotation Sums of Squared Loadings		
Component	Total	% of Variance	Cumulative %	Total	% of Variance	Cumulative %	Total	% of Variance	Cumulative %
1	2.347	33.524	33.524	2.347	33.524	33.524	2.291	32.726	32.726
2	1.771	25.304	58.828	1.771	25.304	58.828	1.827	26.102	58.828
3	.747	10.675	69.503						
4	.664	9.490	78.993						
5	.603	8.617	87.611						
6	.454	6.480	94.091						
7	.414	5.909	100.000						

Note: Extraction method: principal component analysis.

Figure 8.9 Exploratory factor analysis, output II.

variance, an index considered good. The scree graph (Figure 8.10) indicates the retention of three factors, where the line makes the elbow. Combining the two criteria, eigenvalues or latent roots greater than 1, and explained variance close to .6, we will disregard the scree plot, resulting in the extraction of two factors.

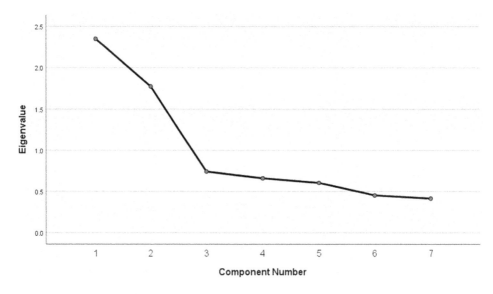

Figure 8.10 Exploratory factor analysis, output III.

	Initial	Extraction
Product variety	1.000	.463
Product quality	1.000	.629
Product availability	1.000	.554
Complaints handling	1.000	.626
Perishable products' quality	1.000	.586
Opening hours	1.000	.699
Lowest price guarantee (financial refund if cheaper product is found)	1.000	.562

Note: Extraction method: principal component analysis.

Figure 8.11 Exploratory factor analysis, output IV.

The communalities indicate the variables' variance shared with the factor solution. All but one reach the acceptable minimum value of .5; however, none reaches the ideal of .7 ($.7^2 \approx .5$, which means that half variance is shared).

The factor loadings indicate the components of each factor. After rotation, using the Varimax method, the loads are better distributed, with v_2, v_8, v_{14}, and v_{30} composing factor 1. Factor 2 is composed of v_{29}, v_{31}, and v_{32}. All variables have high factor loadings, indicating a high correlation with the respective factors.

Now, the factors must be named. The first is composed of product variety (v2), product quality (v8), product availability (v14), and perishable product quality (v30). It could be called the product factor. The second is made up of complaint handling (v29), opening hours (v31), and lowest price guarantee (v32), which could be called the service factor.

Rotated Component Matrix[a]

	Component	
	1	2
Product variety	.652	
Product quality	.793	
Product availability	.736	
Complaints handling		.789
Perishable products' quality	.765	
Opening hours		.831
Lowest price guarantee (financial refund if cheaper product is found)		.679

Notes: Extraction method: Principal component analysis. Rotation method: Varimax with Kaiser Normalization.
a. Rotation converged in three iterations.

Figure 8.12 Exploratory factor analysis, output V.

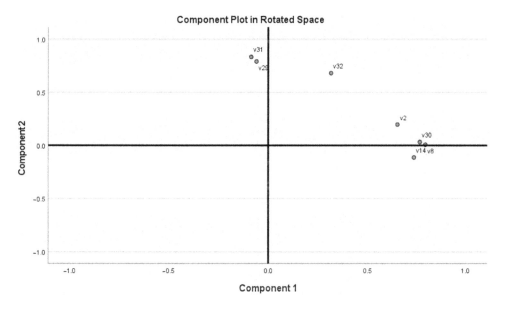

Figure 8.13 Exploratory factor analysis, output VI.

Reliability of the factorial solution

Once the factors are named, we need to check the reliability, unidimensionality, and validity of the factorial solution. Reliability is achieved by calculating Cronbach's alpha coefficient. The sequence in SPSS is:

1   Analyze;
2   Scale;
3   Reliability Analysis;

4 Select items (which would be v2, v8, v14, v30 for the first factor, and v29, v31, v32 for the second);

5 OK.

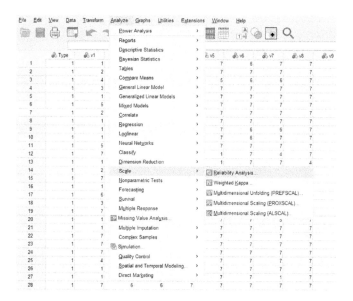

Figure 8.14 Exploratory factor analysis, reliability, I.

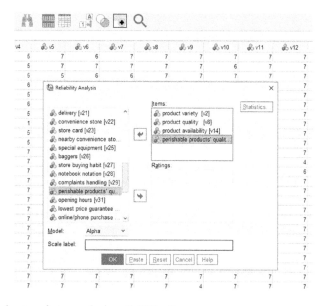

Figure 8.15 Exploratory factor analysis, reliability, II.

Cronbach's Alpha	N of Items
.714	4

Figure 8.16 Exploratory factor analysis, reliability, output I.

Cronbach's Alpha	N of Items
.650	3

Figure 8.17 Exploratory factor analysis, reliability, output II.

Based on the results, the coefficient is .714 for factor 1, higher than the suggested minimum limit, and .650 for factor 2, also above the acceptable limit of 0.6. In this case, the lower coefficient may be due to the small number of indicators in the construct.

Validity of the factorial solution

In order to perform convergent and discriminant validity tests, we need to save our factorial solutions as new variables in the SPSS spreadsheet. This can be done by adding an additional step 9 to the factor analysis sequence in SPSS:

1   Analyze;
2   Dimension Reduction;
3   Factor;
4   Select variables (v2, v8, v14, v29, v30, v31, v32);
5   Descriptives:

    a   Choose Initial solution;
    b   Choose KMO and Bartlett's test of sphericity;
    c   Continue;

6   Extraction:

    a   Choose Principal components (this is the default);
    b   Choose Scree plot;
    c   Continue;

7   Rotation:

    a   Choose Method Varimax;
    b   Choose Display: Rotated solution, Loading plot(s);
    c   Continue;

8   Options:

    a   Choose Sorted by size;
    b   Choose Suppress small coefficients; absolute values less than (.4 or .3);
    c   Continue;

9   Scores:

    a   Choose Save as variables;
    b   Continue;

10 OK.

By doing so, the two factors will appear as additional variables at the end of the data sheet.

The factors created in the previous sequence then need to be compared with the arithmetic mean of the variables that make up the factor.

These can be calculated with the following procedure:

1   Transform;
2   Compute Variable;
3   Target variable:

    a   Create name (e.g. ss1 for the first and ss2 for the second set);

4   Numeric expression:

    a   Here, for the first set: mean (v2, v8, v14, v30);
    b   And for the second set: mean (v29, v31, v32);

5   OK.

After creating the variables *ss1* and *ss2*, we compute the correlation coefficient between the factor scores and the summated scales, following the steps:

1   Analyze;
2   Correlate;

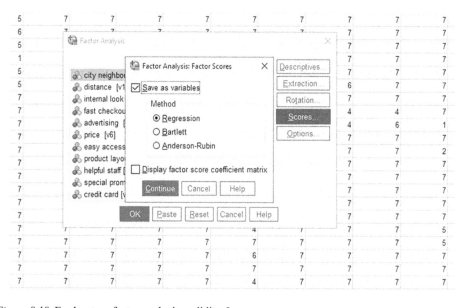

Figure 8.18 Exploratory factor analysis, validity, I.

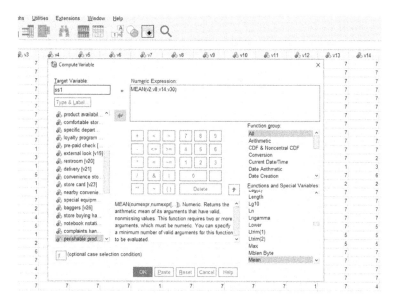

Figure 8.19 Exploratory factor analysis, validity, II.

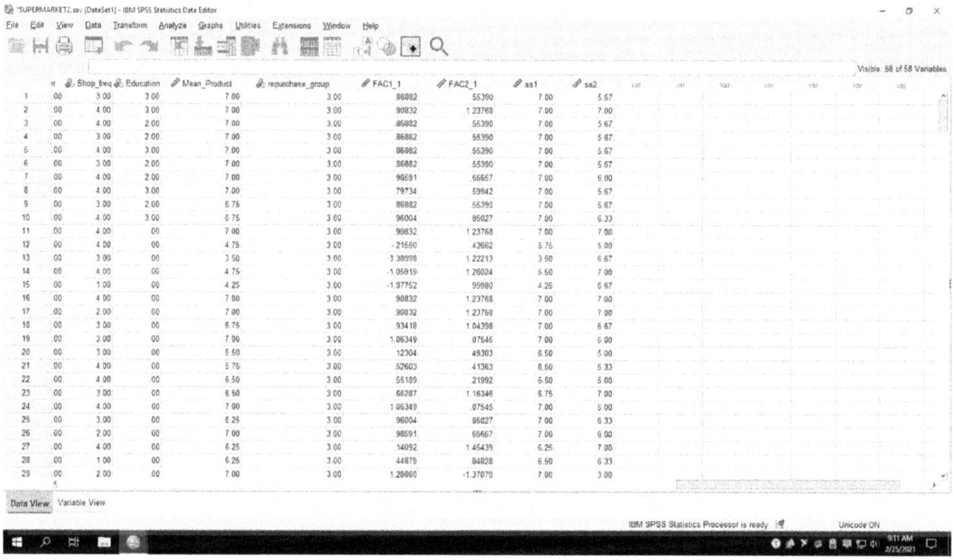

Figure 8.20 Exploratory factor analysis, validity, III.

3 Bivariate;
4 Select variables;
5 OK.

The correlation matrix is presented in Figure 8.23. The convergent validity is confirmed by the high correlation coefficient between factor score 1 and summated scale 1 (.989), and

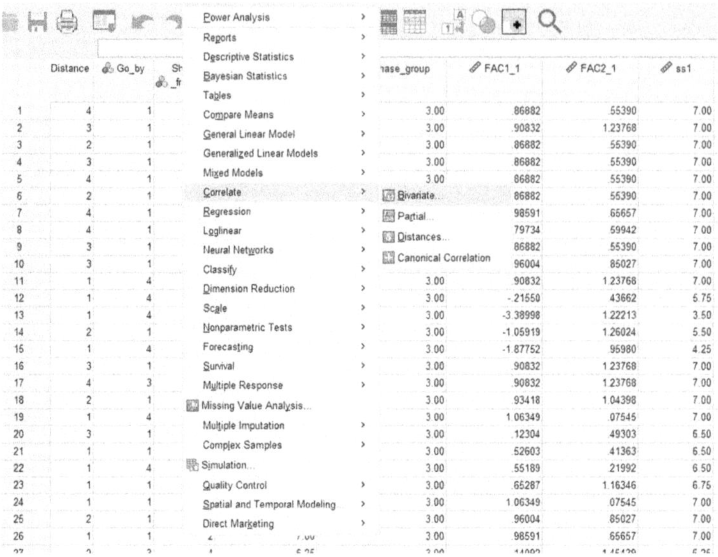

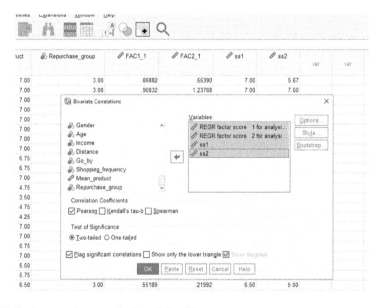

Figure 8.21 Exploratory factor analysis, validity, IV.

Figure 8.22 Exploratory factor analysis, validity, V.

factor score 2 and summated scale 2 (.987), respectively, significant at 1% level. This means that both the factor score and the summated scale are measuring the same dimension, which confirms convergent validity of each factor.

The discriminant validity is confirmed by the low correlations between factor score 1 and summated scale 2, .093; and factor score 2 and summated scale 1, .033. Because of this low correlation, we can conclude that factor 1 and 2 are really unrelated, that is, each factor measures its own concept.

		REGR Factor Score 1 for Analysis 1	REGR Factor Score 2 for Analysis 1	ss1	ss2
REGR factor score 1 for analysis 1	Pearson Correlation	1	.000	.989**	.093
	Sig. (2-tailed)		1.000	.000	.108
	N	300	300	300	300
REGR factor score 2 for analysis 1	Pearson Correlation	.000	1	.033	.987**
	Sig. (2-tailed)	1.000		.564	.000
	N	300	300	300	300
ss1	Pearson Correlation	.989**	.033	1	.115*
	Sig. (2-tailed)	.000	.564		.047
	N	300	300	300	300
ss2	Pearson Correlation	.093	.987**	.115*	1
	Sig. (2-tailed)	.108	.000	.047	
	N	300	300	300	300

** Correlation is significant at the 0.01 level (2-tailed).
* Correlation is significant at the 0.05 level (2-tailed).

Figure 8.23 Exploratory factor analysis, validity, output.

	Initial Eigenvalues			Extraction Sums of Squared Loadings		
Component	Total	% of Variance	Cumulative %	Total	% of Variance	Cumulative %
1	2.211	55.265	55.265	2.211	55.265	55.265
2	.740	18.490	73.755			
3	.620	15.494	89.249			
4	.430	10.751	100.000			

Note: Extraction method: principal component analysis.

Figure 8.24 Exploratory factor analysis, unidimensionality, output I.

The content or face validity is verified by a qualitative assessment of the meaning of the variables forming each construct. For factor 1, there are product variety, product quality, product availability, and perishable product quality, all related to "product." Factor 2 combines the variables complaint handling, opening hours, and lowest price guarantee; all can be referred to as "service." Hence, the variables involved in each factor seem to make sense, which makes the two factors quite appropriate.

Unidimensionality of the factorial solution

Finally, unidimensionality can be assessed by estimating a factor analysis for each construct, containing only its variables. The solution must indicate the extraction of a single construct, with high explained variance. The steps are the same as the steps for the exploratory factor analysis at the beginning of section 8.3, but only the variables of each factor should be selected. For instance, for the first factor, only select v2, v8, v14, and v30.

	Initial Eigenvalues			Extraction Sums of Squared Loadings		
Component	Total	% of Variance	Cumulative %	Total	% of Variance	Cumulative %
1	1.797	59.913	59.913	1.797	59.913	59.913
2	.712	23.750	83.662			
3	.490	16.338	100.000			

Note: Extraction method: principal component analysis.

Figure 8.25 Exploratory factor analysis, unidimensionality, output II.

Kaiser–Meyer–Olkin Measure of Sampling Adequacy.		.717
Bartlett's Test of Sphericity	Approx. Chi-Square	506.765
	df	78
	Sig.	.000

Figure 8.26 Exploratory factor analysis, exercise I.

Based on the results for the first data series, we observe that a single factor, with an eigenvalue greater than 1, was extracted with an explained variance of 55.265% (Figure 8.24). The same can be concluded for factor 2, with a single factor and an explained variance of 59.913% (Figure 8.25). These results attest the constructs' unidimensionality, that is, there is no underlying dimension that can still be extracted.

Exercise

A university board conducted a research to identify factors driving library usage by students. Students answered a questionnaire with 13 variables, and an EFA was performed. The results are in Figures 8.26 *through* 8.29.

1   Is the data suitable for an EFA?
2   How many factors should be retained? Is the explained variance high enough?
3   Are all variables acceptable components for your factors?
4   Analyze and name the factors.
5   Based on your library usage, are they meaningful?

Market insight

Service quality is a well-studied topic in the marketing literature, and several scales were developed to measure it, among them SERVQUAL and SERVPERF. However, each service provider faces different aspects regarding customers preferences. Considering this, propose a survey to measure the service quality of a buffet restaurant located in the business neighborhood of a big city.

1   List the possible factors affecting service quality.
2   List some indicators for each factor.
3   Which factor would be the most important according to the customer's point of view?

	Initial	Extraction
v1	1.000	.565
v2	1.000	.539
v3	1.000	.396
v4	1.000	.418
v5	1.000	.617
v6	1.000	.675
v7	1.000	.598
v8	1.000	.570
v9	1.000	.573
v10	1.000	.463
v11	1.000	.559
v12	1.000	.658
v13	1.000	.625

Note: Extraction method: principal component analysis.

Figure 8.27 Exploratory factor analysis, exercise II.

	Initial Eigenvalues			Extraction Sums of Squared Loadings		
Component	Total	% of Variance	Cumulative %	Total	% of Variance	Cumulative %
1	2.782	21.403	21.403	2.782	21.403	21.403
2	2.006	15.431	36.834	2.006	15.431	36.834
3	1.343	10.330	47.164	1.343	10.330	47.164
4	1.125	8.651	55.815	1.125	8.651	55.815
5	.866	6.663	62.478			
6	.765	5.884	68.362			
7	.758	5.832	74.194			
8	.684	5.262	79.455			
9	.674	5.185	84.641			
10	.589	4.529	89.170			
11	.519	3.989	93.159			
12	.462	3.557	96.716			
13	.427	3.284	100.000			

Note: Extraction method: principal component analysis.

Figure 8.28 Exploratory factor analysis, exercise III.

Rotated Component Matrix[a]

	Component			
	1	2	3	4
1. The teachers you had in the course of your school life had the habit of attending the library.			.735	
2. Since you were a child you were encouraged to acquire the habit of reading.			.695	
3. Computers are available in the library to consult the collection database.	.598			
4. Among the journals available in the library, there are titles in the area that you are most interested in.	.612			
5. Whenever you needed to go to the library to do some research or reading, you found bibliographic material with the answers to your questions.	.762			
6. The teachers always encouraged you to go to the library in search of answers to your doubts regarding the subjects covered in the classroom.			.736	
7. The library's opening hours are consistent with your availability.		.765		
8. The library collection has a sufficient number of titles and copies to suit all users	.754			
9. You have the habit of buying books and magazines.				.736
10. You know all the services the library offers.		.642		
11. You have the habit of "downloading" books over the Internet.				.725
12. You have the habit of reading daily.				.664
13. You, by yourself, are able to find material in the library.		.758		

Note: Extraction method: principal component analysis. Rotation method: Varimax with Kaiser Normalization.
a. Rotation converged in five iterations.

Figure 8.29 Exploratory factor analysis, exercise IV.

Suggested readings

Anderson, R. E., & Srinivasan, S. S. (2003). E-satisfaction and e-loyalty: A contingency frame-work. *Psychology & Marketing, 20*(2), 123–138.

Bian, Q., & Forsythe, S. (2012). Purchase intention for luxury brands: A cross cultural compari-son. *Journal of Business Research, 65*(10), 1443–1451.

Colgate, M., & Lang, B. (2001). Switching barriers in consumer markets: An investigation of the financial services industry. *Journal of Consumer Marketing*, *18*(4), 332–347.

Papadopoulos, N., Martín, O. M., Cleveland, M., & Laroche, M. (2011). Identity, demographics, and consumer behaviors. *International Marketing Review*, *28*(3), 244–266.

Santonen, T. (2007). Price sensitivity as an indicator of customer defection in retail banking. *International Journal of Bank Marketing*, *25*(1), 39–55.

Singh, J. (1990). A typology of consumer dissatisfaction response styles. *Journal of Retailing*, *66*(1), 57.

Vigneron, F., & Johnson, L. W. (2004). Measuring perceptions of brand luxury. *Journal of Brand Management*, *11*(6), 484–506.

9 Confirmatory Factor Analysis (CFA)

Exploratory Factor Analysis (EFA), described in the previous chapter, serves to identify the number of factors that best describes the relations in the data. Thus, the theory is not known or not specified, and EFA helps with theory development. All measured variables are related to all factors by a loading estimate, and the factors are derived from statistical results.

Confirmatory Factor Analysis (CFA), on the other hand, provides confirmation of a model. In other words, the researcher should establish a priori the number of factors and the variables assigned to each factor. Imagine the example of switching intention. The researcher might assume that it could best be described by two factors named complaint satisfaction and failure severity. Another example could be store loyalty, assumed to be described by two factors: product variety and service level. CFA is then used to test whether the hypothesized relations can actually be confirmed with the data. So the researcher designs the model first and then tries to validate it with data that he subsequently collects with primary research.

Section 9.1 explains theoretical backgrounds of CFA, and section 9.2 explores the application of CFA in marketing. Section 9.3 introduces the application of CFA with software specifically dedicated to CFA. An extensive illustration of the application follows in sections 9.4 (modeling), 9.5 (analysis), and 9.6 (output).

9.1 Theoretical background – confirmatory factor analysis

CFA shows how well the factor structure that the researcher had in mind matches the actual data. Thus, it helps to confirm or refuse the proposed theory. As an illustration, let's take Figure 9.1, which shows an example of a theoretical model.

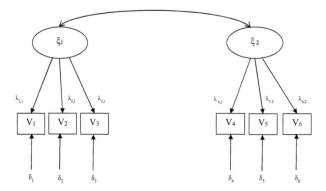

Figure 9.1 A theoretical model.

DOI: 10.4324/9781003196617-9

In this figure, ξ_1 and ξ_2 represent the latent constructs (we use the terms factor and construct interchangeably), v_1–v_6 are the measured variables, $\lambda_{1,1}$–$\lambda_{6,2}$ are the factor loadings, which measure the relationship between the latent constructs and its respective indicators, and δ_1–δ_6 represent the error, or the indicators' variance not explained by the latent construct.

Thus, the model can be represented by a series of equations of the form: $v_1 = \lambda_{v1,1}\,\xi_1\,\delta_1$.

CFA consists of the following steps:

1   Design of the model (as in this example);
2   Estimation of the parameters in the model (such as factor loadings and error terms);
3   Verification of the model fit;
4   Analysis of reliability and validity of the model.

The model fit is a topic that did not achieve consensus in the specific literature yet. There are many indicators for this purpose (Hair et al., 2005; Maroco, 2003; Sharma, 1996), ranging from fit tests to quality of fit measures (absolute, incremental, and parsimony). The measures that are proposed in literature, with their threshold values, are shown in Table 9.1.

The most common fit test is the $\chi2$ significance, which tests if the sample and the estimated covariance matrix are equal. A small (insignificant) $\chi2$ value indicates a good match between the observed results in the sample and the theoretical structure (the estimated covariance matrix), hence a good fit. This would be the case with p values higher than 0.05. However, $\chi2$ increases with a larger sample size, reaching statistical significance even if the difference between the matrices remains the same, thus becoming less useful when used alone. Hair

Table 9.1 Fit Indices

Statistic	Reference Value[1]
Absolute Fit Indices	
Show how well the specified model reproduces the observed data	
$\chi2$ *Goodness-of-Fit*	$p > .05$
$\chi2$ *Goodness-of-Fit corrected for the degrees of freedom* ($\chi2/df$)	*The smaller the better; from 2–5 is acceptable*
Goodness-of-Fit Index (GFI)	$GFI > .90$
Root Mean Square Error of Approximation (RMSEA)	*RMSEA from .05–.08 is acceptable; $< .05$ good fit*
Incremental Fit Indices	
Assess how well a specified model fits relative to some baseline model. The most common baseline model is called null model, which assumes that all observable variables are uncorrelated.	
Normed Fit Index (NFI)	$NFI \geq .92$
Comparative Fit Index (CFI)	$CFI \geq .92$
Tucker Lewis Index (TLI)	$TLI \geq .92$
Relative Fit Index (RFI)	$RFI \geq .92$
Parsimony Fit Indices[2]	
Shows which model, among a set of competitive models, present the best fit. These indices can be improved by either a better fit or a simpler model.	
Parsimony *Comparative Fit Index (PCFI)*	*PCFI from .6–.8, or higher*
Parsimony *Goodness-of-Fit Index (PGFI)*	*PGFI from .6–.8, or higher*
Parsimony *Normed Fit Index (PNFI)*	*PNFI from .6–.8, or higher*

1 Based on Hair et al. (2005) and Maroco (2003).
2 Some authors suggest the use of parsimony indices only for comparison between models, while others recommend their use to evaluate one simple model, as they penalize the complexity.

et al. (2005) recommend the use of multiple indices, at least one of each category, to provide evidences of the model fit.

After confirming the overall model fit, we must verify its reliability and validity. In order to test reliability, we assess Cronbach's alpha and the Composite Reliability Index, which can be estimated using the following formula. The reliability is confirmed if both indices are higher than .7.

$$CR = \frac{\left(\sum_{i=1}^{n} \lambda_i\right)^2}{\left(\sum_{i=1}^{n} \lambda_i\right)^2 + \left(\sum_{i=0}^{n} \delta_i\right)}$$

Where: λ = standardized factor loadings and δ = error term.

To attest validity, there are two different tests, convergent and discriminant validity, both explained in Chapter 6. The convergent validity is attested if the loadings values are greater than .707 and significant at .05. A factor loading of at least 0.707 implies that at least half of the variance of the factor is shared with the construct: $(.707)^2 = 0.5$.

Moreover, the average variance extracted (AVE) should be greater than .5. The AVE can be estimated with the following formula:

$$AVE = \frac{\sum_{i=1}^{n} \lambda^2}{\sum_{i=1}^{n} \lambda^2 + \sum_{i=1}^{n} \delta^2}$$

Where: λ = standardized factor loadings and δ = error term.

The discriminant validity can be tested by using the Fornell–Larcker criterion. According to this criterion, the square root of the AVE of a factor must be higher than the correlation coefficient between two factors.

9.2 Marketing application of CFA

All examples given for Exploratory Factor Analysis (EFA) can be used to illustrate Confirmatory Factor Analysis (CFA). The differences lie in the main purpose. While EFA groups the variables in factors, CFA measures the strength of the factor solution.

An example is the brand personality framework (Aaker, 1997). Based on EFA, Aaker found that there are five dimensions (factors) composing brand personality: sincerity, excitement, competence, sophistication, and ruggedness. For instance, in the brand personality of BMW, excitement is a strong dimension, whereas for Gucci, sophistication is an important element of the brand personality. Aaker composed this brand personality framework based on a sample with respondents from the United States around 25 years ago. If you wish to confirm whether this framework still holds in the current, more digitalized, society, or if you wish to confirm if brand personality has the same structure in another country (let's say France), then CFA is the appropriate technique. For instance, the researcher in France would start with creating a theoretical brand personality model according to the specifications from Aaker's original research in 1997 and then check if the data collected from a French sample match with this original structure. If so, the brand personality framework is validated for France. If not, a new framework would have to be developed for France.

9.3 Application of confirmatory factor analysis with AMOS

For the application of CFA, we use the Gym database. We assume a factor solution with three factors:

- Complaint Management Satisfaction (CS);
- Failure Severity (FS);
- Switching Intention (SI).

In the following, we explore this solution and verify if it can be confirmed. The software to be used is AMOS, included in IBM SPSS Statistics Software (SPSS).
   To perform the analysis, the following activities need to be done:

1   Construct the model (section 9.4);
2   Set up the properties for the analysis (section 9.5);
3   Analysis of output (section 9.6).

You can use the following workshop as guideline for your analysis.

Readers workshop

a   Open the gym database;
b   Perform the analysis;
c   Check normality and the existence of outliers;
d   Check the loadings significance;
e   Check the model fit;
f   Check modification indexes;
g   Correct the model, check model fit;
h   Check reliability (perform reliability analysis);
i   Check validity (convergent, discriminant, and face).

9.4 The CFA model in AMOS

Many activities in AMOS can be done in two ways: with the menu at the top of the screen or with the pictograms at the left of the screen. The sequence of steps here follows the menu at the top of the screen; the figures illustrate the same sequence of steps, but then by indicating the pictograms (buttons) at the left-hand side of the screen.

1   Open AMOS;
2   Draw the diagrams. You need to draw three diagrams, one for each factor (CS, FS, and SI). We start with CS (Complaint Management Satisfaction). CS is a latent (unobserved variable) measured by four statements (observed variables/indicator variables) in the database:

   a   Use "Diagram – Draw Indicator Variable" to design a diagram with four indicator variables. By clicking repeatedly, additional indicator variables are added to the model. For CS, you need four indicator variables in the diagram. AMOS also draws automatically the error terms for each indicator variable.
   b   You can also do this manually by using the pictograms: draw a latent variable or add an indicator to a latent variable, by clicking repeatedly. Remember that the arrows

always point towards the squares (observed variables) in the diagram. Use "Edit" to change format or other properties in your diagram.

3   Select Data File:

    a   "File";
    b   "Data Files";
    c   "File Name" (and then open the Gym database from your laptop or desktop);
    d   Choose "View Data" if you wish to see the data in the file. View Data displays the data in the same style as the SPSS spreadsheet;
    e   OK;

4   Link the diagram you created with the data in the Gym database:

    a   "View" ';
    b   "Variables in Data set";
    c   Assign the indicators to your diagram: drag cs1 to your first box, cs2 to your second box, etc.;

5   Name the latent variable:

    a   Double-click on the circle for the latent variable and the Object Properties appear;
    b   Choose Variable Name "CS";

6   Repeat the procedure for FS (five indicator variables) and SI (four indicator variables);
7   Name the error terms:

    a   "Plugins";
    b   "Name Unobserved Variables";

8   Select the latent variables:

    a   "Edit';
    b   "Select", then click on CS, FS and SI;

9   Create the model by connecting the three latent variables:

    a   "Plugins";
    b   "Draw Covariances";

10   Save the model:

    a   "File";
    b   "Save" (or "Save as").

9.5 The CFA analysis

There are several estimations techniques, AMOS offers five options. The most common is maximum likelihood estimation (MLE), which is suitable for the sample size we are using. The other options apply when any violations are found or according to specific characteristics of the sample or sample size.

The estimation requires the following steps:

1   View:

    a   Analysis Properties – Estimation:

        Select Maximum likelihood (default);

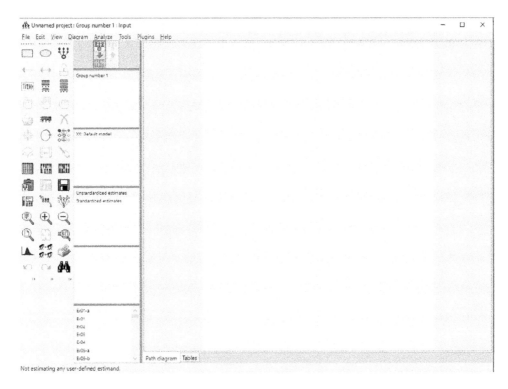

Figure 9.2 The AMOS worksheet.

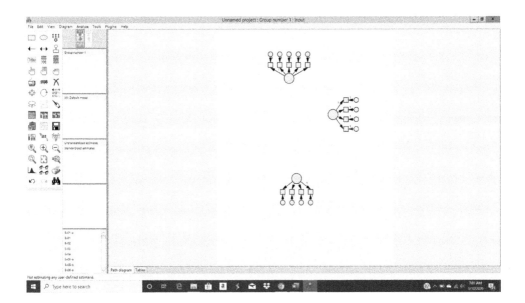

Figure 9.3 Three diagrams in AMOS.

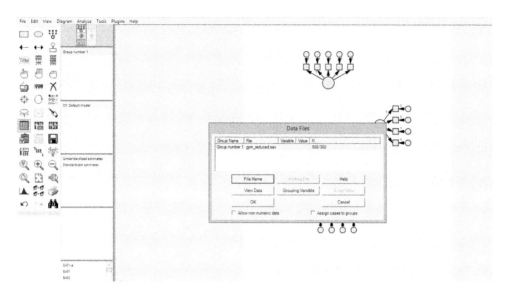

Figure 9.4 Select data file (SPSS database).

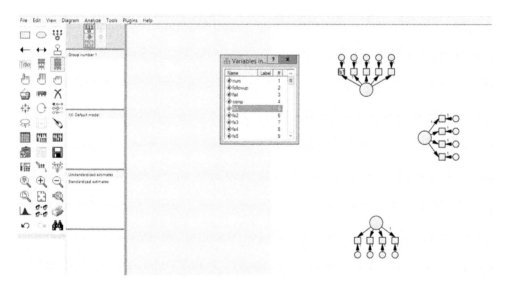

Figure 9.5 Assign indicators.

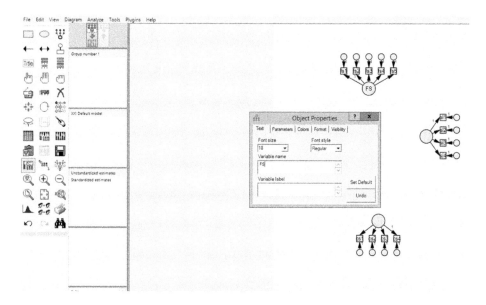

Figure 9.6 Name latent variables.

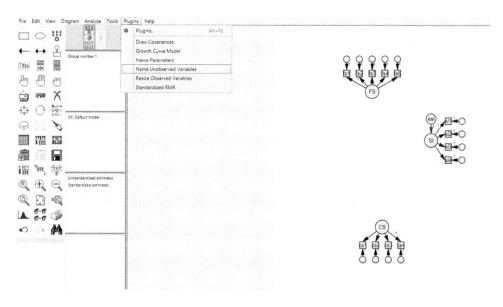

Figure 9.7 Name error terms.

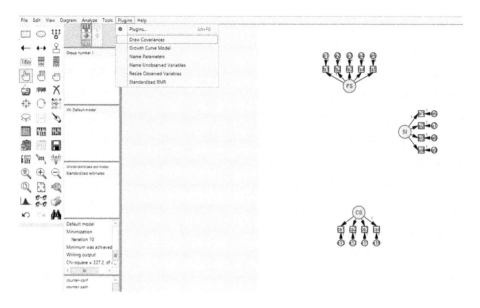

Figure 9.8 Select latent variables.

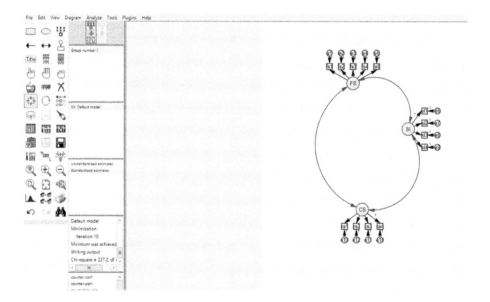

Figure 9.9 Draw covariances.

b   Analysis Properties – Output:

    i   Select Minimization history (default);
    ii   Select Standardized Estimates;
    iii   Select Modification Indices;
    iv   Select tests for normality and outliers;

2   Analyze:

a   Calculate Estimates;

3   Switch view to Output Path Diagrams, and select Standardized Estimates.

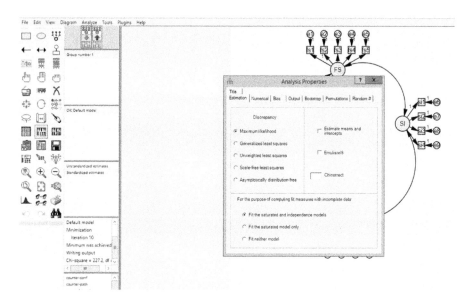

Figure 9.10 Analysis properties – estimates.

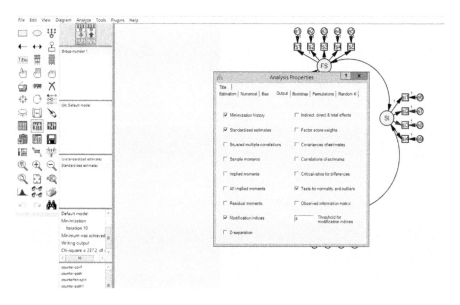

Figure 9.11 Analysis properties – output.

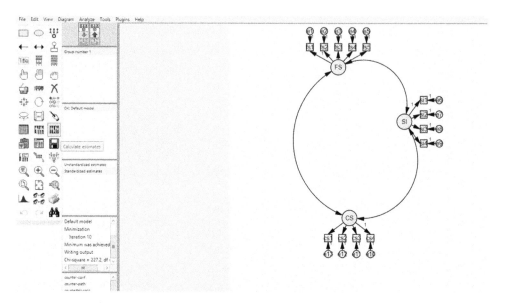

Figure 9.12 Run the analysis – calculate estimates.

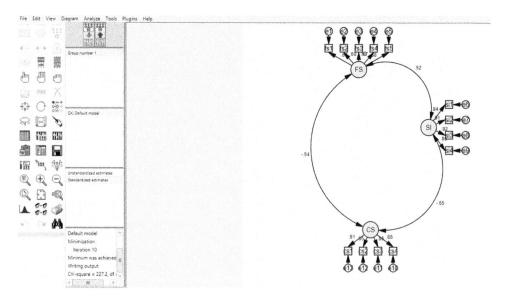

Figure 9.13 Output path diagram with standardized estimates of loadings and coefficients.

9.6 The CFA output

With "*View – Text Output*" you get Notes for Model. This output shows some information about the model. This information essentially is a summary of the model fit in Figure 9.14 and will be explained in more detail there.

In some situations, the model will not be estimated. That requires the identification of the problem and most likely a change of the model or one of its parameters.

Next, we turn to *"Assessment of normality"* (see Figure 9.15). Normality is realized if the kurtosis statistic is smaller than the critical ratio (c.r.). Although most variables present univariate normality, the multivariate normality was not achieved, as the kurtosis statistic (82.986) falls beyond the critical ratio (36.392). We will proceed with the analysis based on

Figure 9.14 AMOS output – notes for model.

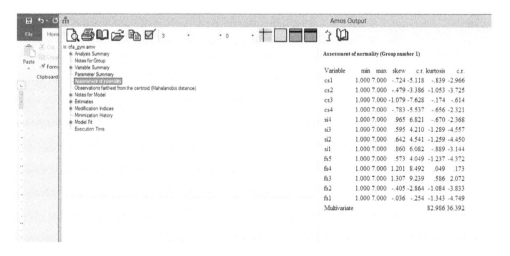

Figure 9.15 AMOS output – assessment of normality.

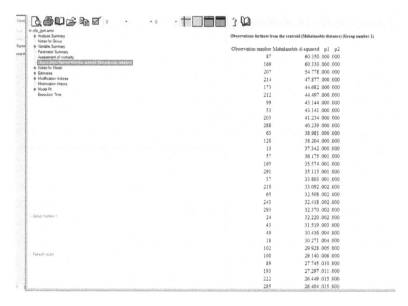

Figure 9.16 AMOS output – outliers.

the univariate normality, and mostly because the sample size is big (the multivariate normality statistics are sensitive to big samples).

Outliers can be identified with *"Observations farthest from the centroid (Mahalanobis distance)"*. The sample contains 13 multivariate outliers, if we take *p*1 smaller than 0.001 as the criterion. Outliers could worsen the results, but they could also represent specific features of the respondents. In this analysis, we choose to keep them.

In the *"Estimates"* (Figure 9.17) we can observe the estimated unstandardized and standardized factor loadings (standardized regression weights). The standardized factor loadings were also visible in the output path diagram (Figure. 9.13).

All measured variables are significant for the model, with a significance level of 0.000 (***), and standardized values above 0.5, although some did not achieve the ideal threshold value of 0.707.

The *"Model Fit"* (Figures 9.18 and 9.19) gives information about relevant fit indicators. In general terms, the model fit is not quite good:

- The ρ is significant (also visible in Figure 9.14);
- The $\chi 2/df$ *(CMIN/DF)* is 3.665, (between 2–5, acceptable);
- The GFI is below 0.9, (should be $\geq$ .90);
- The RMSEA is .094 (.05–.08).

The incremental indices (CFI, TLI, and NFI) and the parsimony indices (PCFI and PNFI) are acceptable, as they are above the threshold. (.92 and between .7 and .8, respectively)

Because of the limited model fit, the model needs to be specified again. For this purpose, we need to look at the *"Modification Indices."* We observe (Figure 9.20) that some error terms (pertaining to the same construct) are highly correlated, probably because their

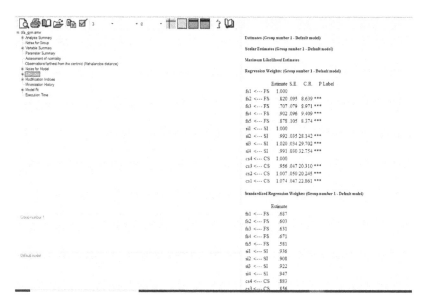

Figure 9.17 AMOS output – estimates.

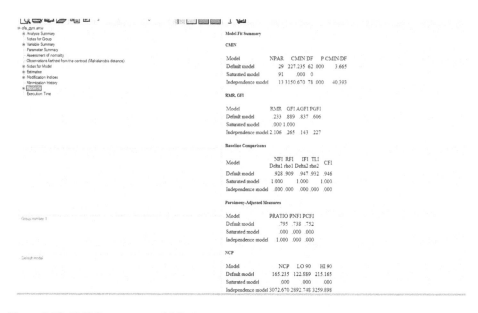

Figure 9.18 AMOS output – model fit, I.

respective indicators are highly correlated as well. Hence, the measures have common specifications, and it is theoretically justifiable to covary them and run the estimation again (for example: e12 and e13, e3 and e4, and e1 and e2).

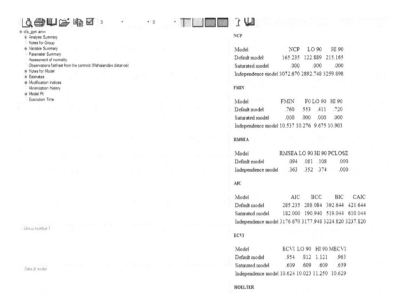

Figure 9.19 AMOS output – model fit, II.

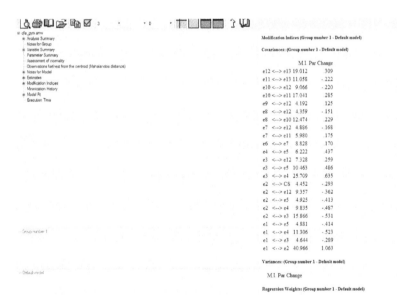

Figure 9.20 AMOS output – modification indices.

In order to covary the error terms, return to the Input Path Diagram, and follow the steps:

1   Diagram;
2   Draw Covariances (double headed arrows) to link the selected error terms (because the program can name the errors in a different manner, the reader should covary the following error pairs: fs1 and fs2; fs3 and fs4; cs1 and cs2);

3   Save file;
4   Run the analysis again, according to the steps specified in section 9.5.

Now, the model presents a better fit (Figures 9.22 and 9.23). The $\chi 2/df$ decreases to 2.214, the GFI is equal .937, and the incremental fit indices are all above .92. The parsimony indices, although reduced, are within their thresholds. Finally, the RMSEA is also acceptable, with a value of .064.

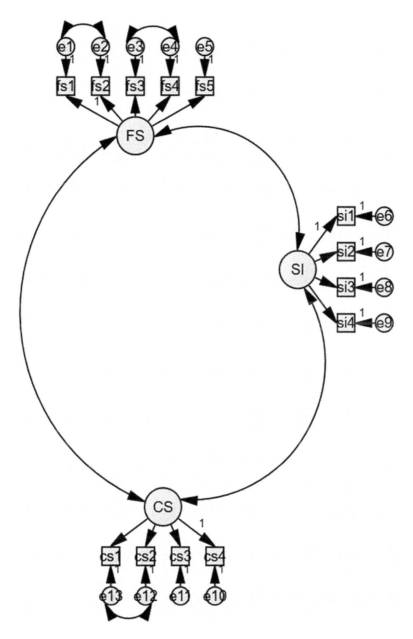

Figure 9.21 Model with correlated error terms.

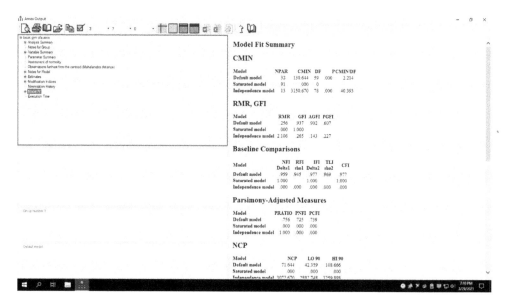

Figure 9.22 AMOS output – model fit, revised model I.

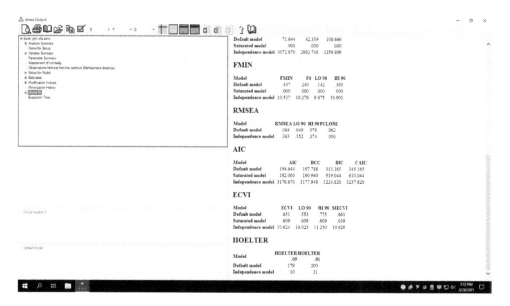

Figure 9.23 AMOS output – model fit, revised model II.

The final step is to check the measurement model reliability and validity. Figures 9.24 and 9.25 show the reliability and validity estimations using an Excel sheet. You have to create the Excel sheet yourself, as AMOS does not provide estimates for reliability and validity. The loadings are the standardized estimates, taken from the AMOS output.

Remember that reliability can be confirmed if CR (Composite Reliability Index) is above .7. This is the case for all three latent variables (FS, CS, and SI).

	Estimate (loadings)	Square1 (loadings)	Sum of square1	AVE (SS/n)	Delta (1-Square1)	Sum of loadings	Square2 Sum of loadings	sum of delta	Denominator square2+ sum of delta	CR square2/ denom
fs1 ← FS	0.614	0.377			0.623					
fs2 ← FS	0.507	0.257			0.743					
fs3 ← FS	0.623	0.388			0.612					
fs4 ← FS	0.670	0.449			0.551					
fs5 ← FS	0.619	0.383	1.854	0.371	0.617	3.033	9.199	3.146	12.345	**0.745**
si1 ← SI	0.937	0.878			0.122					
si2 ← SI	0.907	0.823			0.177					
si3 ← SI	0.922	0.850			0.150					
si4 ← SI	0.947	0.897	3.448	0.862	0.103	3.713	13.786	0.552	14.339	**0.961**
cs4 ← CS	0.908	0.824			0.176					
cs3 ← CS	0.880	0.774			0.226					
cs2 ← CS	0.801	0.642			0.358					
cs1 ← CS	0.867	0.752	2.992	0.748	0.248	3.456	11.944	1.008	12.952	**0.922**

Figure 9.24 Reliability and validity tests.

	FS	SI	CS
FS	**0.609**		
SI	0.515	**0.928**	
CS	−0.540	−0.646	**0.865**

Figure 9.25 Discriminant validity.

Convergent validity is confirmed with AVE higher than .5 and loadings higher than .707. This is the case for CS and SI, but the convergent validity cannot be confirmed for FS. This implies that there is limited correlation between the five indicators used to estimate FS. Based on this outcome, we might advise to change at least some of the statements that are used to measure FS (failure severity).

The discriminant validity is confirmed, as the correlations between constructs are smaller than the square root of their AVE (main diagonal).

Exercises

I. A health care provider conducted a research to evaluate customer satisfaction after a complaint and the respective service recovery. The factors identified are complaint handling satisfaction (CHS); satisfaction with the health provider service (SAT); and loyalty (LOY). The results of a CFA are in Figures 5.26 and 5.27.

1   *Is the factor solution statistically consistent?*
2   *Is the factor solution theoretically consistent?*
3   *Are the fit indexes acceptable?*

DV	IV	Estimate
CHS1. Were you satisfied with the way the company handled your complaint?	CHS	.819
CHS2. Overall, were you satisfied with the response you received to your complaint?	CHS	.835
CHS3. Do you believe that it is worth complaining, since Company X will consider and answer your manifestation?	CHS	.751
LOY1. Do you want to change your health plan?	LOY	.613
LOY2. Would you say positive things about Company X to other people?	LOY	−.927
LOY3. Would you recommend Company X to friends, neighbors and relatives?	LOY	−.972
SAT1. Are you satisfied with the way Company X communicates with you?	SAT	.701
SAT2. Are you, in general, satisfied with Company X?	SAT	.818
SAT3. Is Company X a quality company?	SAT	.844

Figure 9.26 Exercise, I.

Model Fit Summary

CMIN

Model	NPAR	CMIN	DF	P	CMIN/DF
Default model	21	66.625	24	.000	2.776
Saturated model	45	.000	0		
Independence model	9	1521.735	36	.000	42.270

RMR, GFI

Model	RMR	GFI	AGFI	PGFI
Default model	.112	.941	.890	.502
Saturated model	.000	1.000		
Independence model	1.315	.277	.096	.221

Baseline Comparisons

Model	NFI Delta1	RFI rho1	IFI Delta2	TLI rho2	CFI
Default model	.956	.934	.972	.957	.971
Saturated model	1.000		1.000		1.000
Independence model	.000	.000	.000	.000	.000

Parsimony-Adjusted Measures

Model	PRATIO	PNFI	PCFI
Default model	.667	.637	.648
Saturated model	.000	.000	.000
Independence model	1.000	.000	.000

NCP

Model	NCP	LO 90	HI 90
Default model	42.625	22.038	70.862
Saturated model	.000	.000	.000
Independence model	1485.735	1361.809	1617.033

FMIN

Model	FMIN	F0	LO 90	HI 90
Default model	.288	.185	.095	.307
Saturated model	.000	.000	.000	.000
Independence model	6.588	6.432	5.895	7.000

RMSEA

Model	RMSEA	LO 90	HI 90	PCLOSE
Default model	.088	.063	.113	.008
Independence model	.423	.405	.441	.000

AIC

Model	AIC	BCC	BIC	CAIC
Default model	108.625	110.526	181.007	202.007
Saturated model	90.000	94.072	245.103	290.103
Independence model	1539.735	1540.550	1570.756	1579.756

ECVI

Model	ECVI	LO 90	HI 90	MECVI
Default model	.470	.381	.592	.478
Saturated model	.390	.390	.390	.407
Independence model	6.666	6.129	7.234	6.669

Figure 9.27 Exercise, II.

HOELTER

Model	HOELTER .05	HOELTER .01
Default model	127	150
Independence model	8	9

Figure 9.27 (Continued)

Market insight

Phone companies register high churn rates, compared to other service providers, such as fitness center and health care providers. As customer retention is fundamental to these companies, they need to constantly check customer satisfaction and their propensity to leave.

How can a CFA be used in order to prevent churn, or at least identify customers prone to defection?

1   List the possible factors affecting service quality.
2   List some indicators for each factor.
3   Which factor(s) would be the most important to prevent defection?

Suggested readings

Bagozzi, R. P., & Yi, Y. (2012). Specification, evaluation, and interpretation of structural equation models. *Journal of the Academy of Marketing Science, 40*(1), 8–34.

Bian, Q., & Forsythe, S. (2012). Purchase intention for luxury brands: A cross cultural comparison. *Journal of Business Research, 65*(10), 1443–1451.

Griffin, M., Babin, B. J., & Modianos, D. (2000). Shopping values of Russian consumers: The impact of habituation in a developing economy. *Journal of Retailing, 76*(1), 33–52.

Kim, Y. H., Lee, M. Y., & Kim, Y. K. (2011). A new shopper typology: Utilitarian and hedonic perspectives. *Journal of Global Academy of Marketing, 21*(2), 102–113.

Sharma, P., & Chan, R. (2015). Demystifying deliberate counterfeit purchase behaviour: Towards a unified conceptual framework. *Marketing Intelligence and Planning. 34*(3), 318–335.

Strizhakova, Y., Coulter, R. A., & Price, L. L. (2008). Branded products as a passport to global citizenship: Perspectives from developed and developing countries. *Journal of International Marketing, 16*(4), 57–85.

Vigneron, F., & Johnson, L. W. (2004). Measuring perceptions of brand luxury. *Journal of Brand Management, 11*(6), 484–506.

10 Structural Equation Modeling (SEM)

Structural Equation Modeling (SEM) measures the relations between two or more latent variables. SEM examines the structure of interrelations expressed in a series of equations that describe the relationships between the constructs involved in the analysis. If a researcher wants to assess how perceived value (PV) influences satisfaction (SAT) and how both influence loyalty (LOY), it is necessary to estimate one equation for the relation between PV and SAT, one for the relation between PV and LOY, and a third one for SAT and LOY. SEM not only estimates these relations simultaneously but estimates the relations between the constructs and their indicators, as well. An endless list of possible applications of SEM could be made, such as word-of-mouth, attitude, and purchase intention or perceived justice, complaint handling, and switching intention, among others. Obviously, the model is suitable for more than two or three factors. As an example, two well-known models, the American Customer Satisfaction Index (Fornell, Johnson, Anderson, Cha, & Bryant, 1996) and the Key Mediating Variable Model (Morgan & Hunt, 1994), illustrate the purpose of SEM. In the Key Mediating Variable Model, for instance, SEM assesses the interrelations between trust and commitment and their relationship with antecedent and consequent constructs.

Section 10.1 explains the theoretical background of the SEM. Then, a number of marketing applications are described in section 10.2, and a step-by-step description of the application of SEM in AMOS is introduced in section 10.3. An extensive illustration follows in the sections 10.4 (modeling), 10.5 (analysis), and 10.6 (output).

10.1 Theoretical background – structural equation modeling

Figure 10.1 shows a hypothetical model.

The figure consists of two separated parts: the measurement model, below the dashed line, which measures the factors or latent variables, as in confirmatory factor analysis, and the structural model, above the dashed line, which measures the relations between the constructs, as in multiple linear regression.

There are three constructs in the figure: ξ_1, called exogenous because it is not influenced by any other construct, and η_1 and η_2, called endogenous, as they are influenced by other(s) construct(s). The structural model can be represented by the following structural equations:

$$\eta_1 = \lambda_{1,1}\, \xi_1 + \zeta_1$$
$$\eta_2 = \lambda_{2,1}\, \xi_1 + \beta_{2,1}\, \eta_1 + \zeta_2$$

The relations between an exogenous construct and an endogenous construct are quantified by the structural coefficient λ. The relation between the endogenous constructs is represented

DOI: 10.4324/9781003196617-10

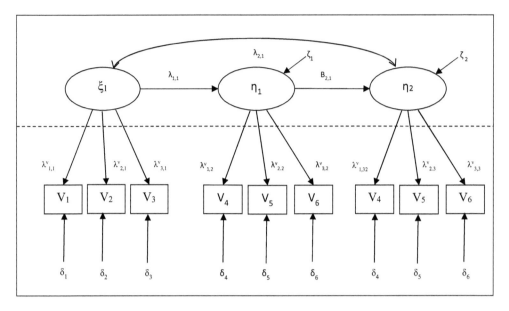

Figure 10.1 Structural equation modeling.

by the structural coefficient β. The first subscript stands for the affected construct and the second for the causal construct. ζ represents the error, or the amount of relationship not explained in the equation. It is important to evaluate not only the relations but also the overall model fit. This can be done with the same fit indices as used in confirmatory factor analysis.

10.2 Marketing application of SEM

Countless models have been proposed in consumer behavior research. Many of these models explain the relationships between latent variables such as brand awareness, brand preference, brand liking, and purchase intention. SEM is useful to explore these models, as it allows the measurement of the relationships between the construct and its indicators and among the constructs themselves.

Loyalty is a central concept in relationship marketing. It is extremely important for service providers, especially the subscription-based ones, and also to retail stores, as it means positive attitude and repeat purchases. Which variables influence loyalty? Depending on the sector, the importance may vary, but normally perceived value, satisfaction, trust, and switching costs have a positive influence. SEM can be used to validate possible relationship marketing models.

In certain occasions, consumers present a high repurchase behavior combined with a low positive attitude toward the provider. This is called inertia. This is a dangerous situation, as it represents a kind of spurious loyalty: whenever a competing opportunity becomes available, the customer will defect. Not to mention that this type of "loyal" customer is often the source of negative word-of-mouth. Among the possible drivers for inertia, there are unattractiveness (or unavailability) of alternative suppliers, customer's perceived risk of switching to another supplier, and switching barriers. SEM could be used to explore possible drivers and their relations.

The sales of counterfeit ("fake") products have been growing fast for many years, despite the risk of getting caught and the campaigns launched by the producers of the original brands emphasizing the risks associated with counterfeiting. What factors positively influence the purchase intention of "fake" brands? There could be social or economic benefits, counterfeit proneness, and brand image, among others. SEM can help in identifying the main drivers in order to mitigate this fraudulent behavior.

Along with the increase in social media, e-commerce has been growing fast in recent periods. Companies are increasingly using this environment to promote their products and services, for instance by using search engine advertising. At the same time, the electronic word-of-mouth communication (e-WOM) is also presenting high growth rates. This involves not only customer comments but also endorsement by social influencers. Among the different types of communication (e.g., brands advertising their own products, e-WOM, and influencers), which one is more trustworthy, and which is more influential in driving purchase intention? SEM can help to explore this.

10.3 Application of structural equation modeling with AMOS

We continue with the same model as used to illustrate confirmatory factor analysis. We continue with the gym database, and focus on the same three factors as in the previous chapter:

- Complaint Management Satisfaction (CS);
- Failure Severity (FS);
- Switching Intention (SI).

In the application, we explore how well CS and FS explain SI. The software is AMOS, included in IBM SPSS Statistics Software (SPSS).

Readers workshop

a   Open the gym database;
b   Perform the analysis, following these steps;
c   Check normality and the existence of outliers (this step was also performed in Chapter 9; it is not shown in the sequence here);
d   Check the path coefficients signal and significance;
e   Check the loadings significance;
f   Check the explained variance;
g   Check the model fit;
h   Check modification indexes;
i   Correct the model, check model fit;
j   Check reliability (perform reliability analysis);
k   Check validity (convergent, discriminant, and face validity).

SEM involves the following stages, which are largely the same as in CFA (see previous chapter):

1   Create structural model (section 10.4);
2   Set up the properties for the analysis (section 10.5);
3   Analysis of output (section 10.6).

10.4 The SEM model in AMOS

In order to create a structural model in SEM, we first need to create the factors (constructs). This is done in exactly the same way as with CFA. Consequently, steps 1 to 7 are identical to steps 1 to 7 in section 9.4. For the reader's convenience, we reprinted these seven steps here:

1   Open AMOS;
2   Draw the diagrams. You need to draw three diagrams, one for each factor (CS, FS, and SI). We start with CS (Complaint Management Satisfaction). CS is a latent (unobserved variable) measured by four statements (observed variables/indicator variables) in the database.

    a   Use "Diagram – Draw Indicator Variable" to design a diagram with four indicator variables. By clicking repeatedly, additional indicator variables are added to the model. For CS, you need four indicator variables in the diagram. AMOS also draws automatically the error terms for each indicator variable.
    b   You can also do this manually by using the pictograms: draw a latent variable or add an indicator to a latent variable by clicking repeatedly. Remember that the arrows always point towards the squares (observed variables) in the diagram. Use "Edit" to change format or other properties in your diagram.

3   Select Data File:

    a   "File";
    b   "Data Files";
    c   "File Name" (and then open the Gym database from your laptop or desktop);
    d   Choose "View Data" if you wish to see the data in the file. View Data displays the data in the same style as the SPSS spreadsheet;
    e   OK;

4   Link the diagram you created with the data in the Gym database:

    a   "View";
    b   "Variables in Data set";
    c   Assign the indicators to your diagram: drag cs1 to your first box, cs2 to your second box, etc.;

5   Name the latent variable:

    a   Double-click on the circle for the latent variable and the Object Properties appear;
    b   Choose Variable Name "CS";

6   Repeat the procedure for FS (five indicator variables) and SI (four indicator variables);
7   Name the error terms:

    a   "Plugins";
    b   "Name Unobserved Variables";

The result of steps 1 to 7 is the following diagram, identical to Figure 9.7 of the previous chapter.

    With CFA, we "simply" covary the three factors (constructs) to find out how they are related (steps 8 to 10 in section 9.4). With SEM, we go a step further: the researcher expects relations between these factors. In our model, the researcher expects that satisfaction about

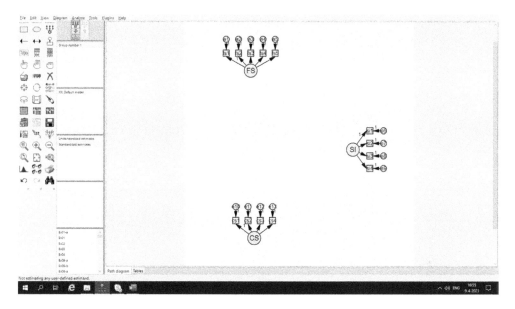

Figure 10.2 The factors of a structural model.

the way complaints were handled (CS) and the severity of the issue (failure severity – FS) have an impact on switching intention (SI). As expressed in the terminology of SEM: the researcher expects a model with two exogenous factors (CS, FS) and one endogenous factor (SI).

In order to create the structural model, after having created the three factors (constructs), we proceed with the following steps:

8   Add error term to the endogenous factor (the factor to be estimated; here, SI):

    a   "Diagram";
    b   "Draw unique variable";
    c   Select the factor to which you want to create the error term (here, SI);

9   Name the error term:

    a   Double-click on the circle for the variable to be named (here: the error term) and the Object Properties appear;
    b   Choose Variable Name "esi";

10   Add structural paths:

    a   "Diagram";
    b   "Draw path";

11   Covary the exogenous factors:

    a   Select the latent variables:

        i   "Edit';
        ii   "Select", then click on CS and FS;

    b   Draw covariance by connecting the two factors:

        i   "Plugins";
        ii   "Draw Covariances";

12 Save the model:

    a   "File";
    b   "Save" (or "Save as").

First, we need to add (Figure 10.3) and name an error term (Figure 10.4) to the endogenous factor SI.

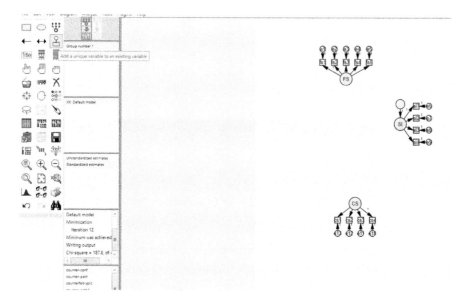

Figure 10.3 Add error term to the endogenous factor.

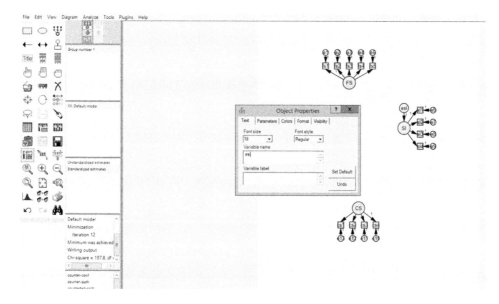

Figure 10.4 Name error term.

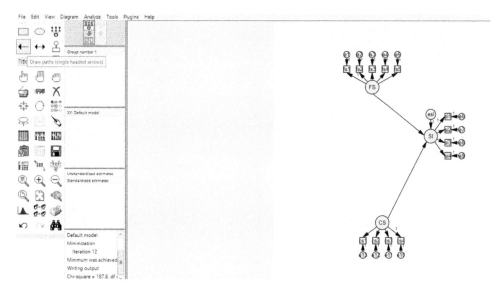

Figure 10.5 Add structural paths.

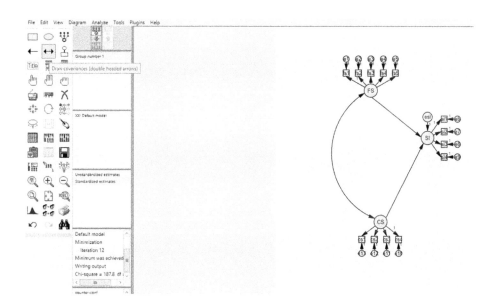

Figure 10.6 Covary the exogenous factors.

Now we add the structural paths (Figure 10.5) from exogenous to endogenous constructs, and then we covary the exogenous constructs (Figure 10.6).

10.5 The SEM analysis

The procedure to create the analysis is similar to the one for CFA (see section 9.5). The only difference is that we want some additional output (see Figure 10.7)

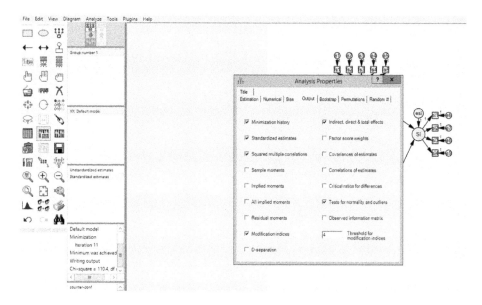

Figure 10.7 Analysis properties.

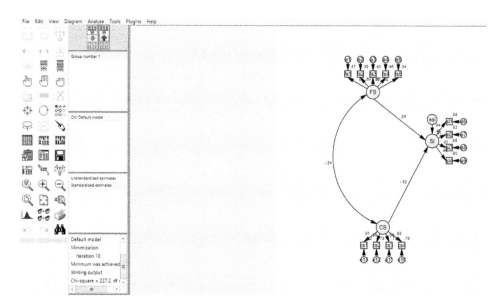

Figure 10.8 Output path diagram with standardized estimates.

Figure 10.8 shows the estimated model. The results show the relations between the three constructs (structural model) and between the constructs and their indicators (measurement model). We observe that FS positively and significantly influences SI and that CS negatively and significantly affects SI. The measurement model is about the same we saw in CFA; all indicators are significant at .000 level.

10.6 The SEM output

As was the case in sections 10.4 and 10.5, the steps and procedures to be followed are largely the same as in the previous chapter. For our explanation, we zoom in on *Estimates, Model Fit* and *Modification Indices*. First, we look at *Estimates*. As showed in Figures 10.9 and 10.10, FS positively influences SI (.241), and CS has a negative effect (–.515), both coefficients are significant.

Figure 10.9 SEM output – Estimates I.

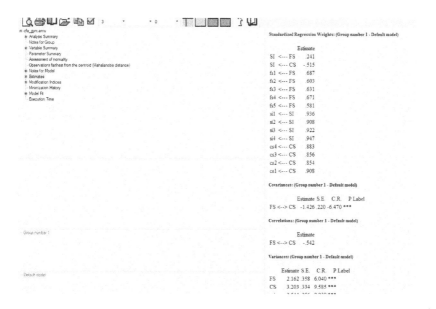

Figure 10.10 AMOS output – Estimates II.

The squared multiple correlations (Figure 10.11a) show that 45.8% of the SI variance is explained by CS and FS.

After showing an overview of the direct effects, the SEM output lists indirect effects (Figure 10.11b). These indirect effects are important when there are constructs mediating the relations. For instance, in the model we used in the introduction of this chapter, perceived value of a brand stimulates satisfaction, which in turn influences brand loyalty (next to a direct effect of perceived value on loyalty).

For the evaluation of the model fit, the same indices as used for CFA should be used. Again, the model fit is not quite good. The indices have identical values as in section 9.6: the

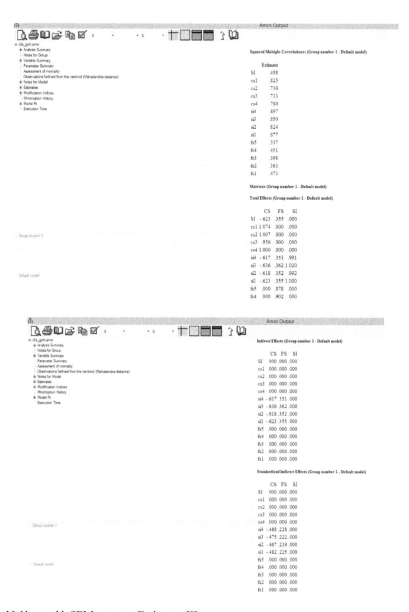

Figure 10.11 a and b SEM output – Estimates III.

ρ is significative (notes for model), the $\chi2/df$ is 3.665, the GFI is below 0.9, and the RMSEA is higher than .8. The incremental indices and the parsimony indices are above the threshold.

Because the fit is not good, the model needs to be specified again. For this purpose, we must observe the modification indices and check if there are error terms highly correlated and if the inclusion of an additional path would reduce the $\chi2$ value. Modifications are only acceptable when based on theoretical reasons, for example, the correlation between the error terms is caused by correlation among their respective variables, or the path to be included is theoretically supported. No additional path is suggested (Figure 10.14). However, we

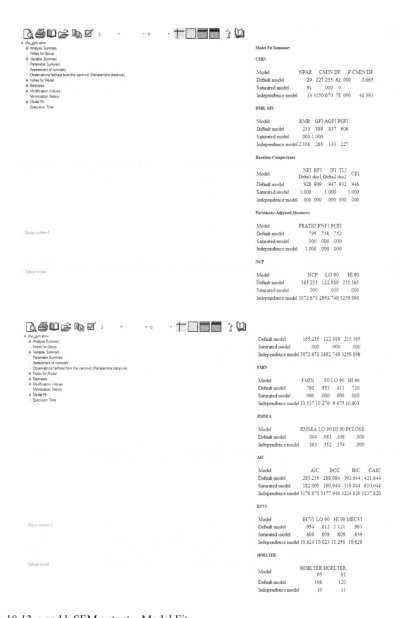

Figure 10.12 a and b SEM output – Model Fit.

observe that errors e12 and e13, e3 and e4, and e1 and e2 are correlated (remember that the same results were found in the CFA output in Chapter 9) and so we must covary them. If this additional covariation would not be enough, we would have to investigate the correlations between measured variables and exclude variables with high correlation coefficients. Additionally, we can exclude variables with low factor loadings.

In order to covary the error terms, we have to follow exactly the same procedure as described in section 9.6 (*Diagram – Draw Covariances – Save File – Run the analysis again*). The resulting model is shown in Figure 10.15.

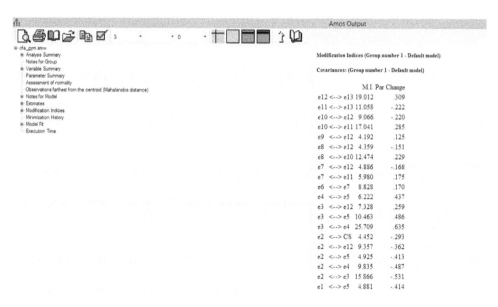

Figure 10.13 SEM output – Modification Indices I.

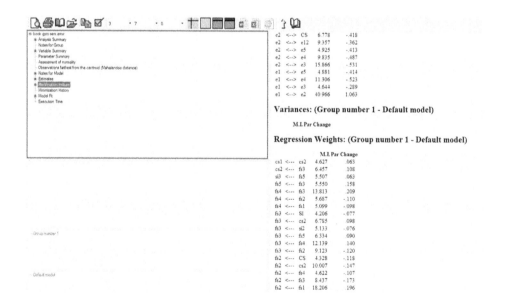

Figure 10.14 SEM output – Modification Indices II.

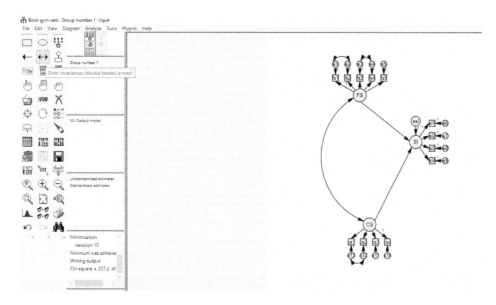

Figure 10.15 SEM model with correlated error terms.

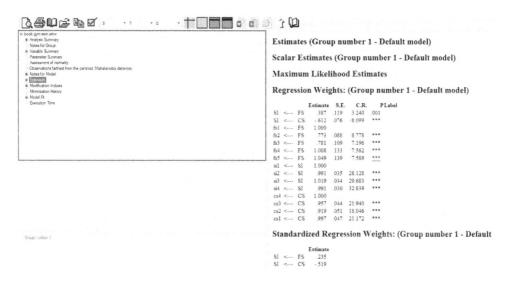

Figure 10.16 SEM output – Estimates, Revised Model I.

After we covary the error terms, the factor loadings and path coefficients are slightly different, but all are significant at .000 level (Figure 10.16). The path structure is in the same direction, and the squared multiple correlation slightly reduced to .456. As in our previous example, the model fit is now better (Figure 10.18). The $\chi2/df$ decreases to 2.214, the GFI is equal .937, and RMSEA is .064. The incremental fit indices are all above .92, and the parsimony indices, although reduced, are within the threshold,

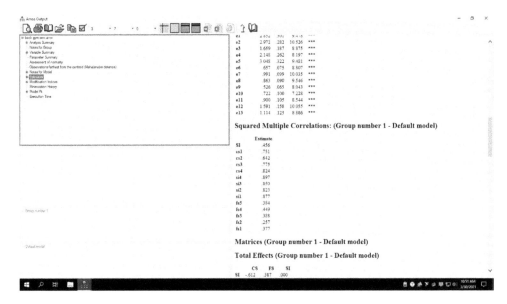

Figure 10.17 SEM output – Estimates, Revised Model II.

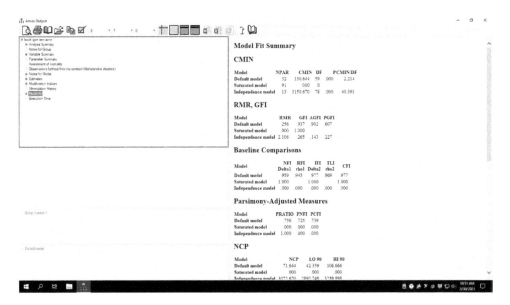

Figure 10.18 a and b SEM output – Model Fit, Revised Model III.

In sum, FS positively influences SI (path coefficient equals .235, with significance .000) and CS negatively influences SI (−.519, sig .000), and both variables together explain almost 46% of SI. Thus, satisfaction with the complaint handling reduces the switching intention, and this effect is stronger than the increase in switching intention due to fail severity. This

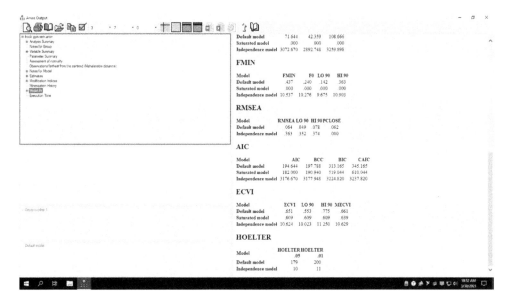

Figure 10.18 (Continued)

result serves a great managerial implication: good service recovery/complaint handling is able to reduce the damage caused by mistakes in the service delivery.

The final step is the measurement model reliability and validity tests, which are exactly the same in the CFA chapter (see Figures 9.23 and 9.24).

Sometimes, the tests of the reliability and validity of the measurement model are presented before the structural results. However, we recommend assessing the structural model (the relations between factors) first. If the structural model needs respecification, then this will change the loadings, possibly even the factors composition (in case strongly correlated variables need to be excluded, for instance). Therefore, it makes sense to first achieve structural fit and only then to look at the reliability and validity of the measurement model.

Exercises

A health care provider conducted a research to evaluate customer satisfaction after a complaint and the respective service recovery. The factors identified are complaint handling satisfaction (CHS); satisfaction with the health provider service (SAT); and loyalty (LOY). A SEM was performed to evaluate the influence of CHS on SAT and the influence of SAT on LOY.

1   Is the measurement model consistent?
2   Are the relationships between constructs statistically significant?
3   Are the fit indexes acceptable?
4   Are the relationships between constructs theoretically consistent? (Tip: analyze the meaning of LOY indicators).

Standardized Regression Weights: (Group number 1 – Default model)

DV		IV	Estimate
SAT		CHS	.757***
LOY		SAT	−.913***
Were you satisfied with the way the company handled your complaint?		CHS	.819***
Overall, were you satisfied with the response you received to your complaint?		CHS	.833***
Do you believe that it is worth complaining, since Company X will consider and answer your manifestation?		CHS	.753***
Do you want to change your health plan?		LOY	.613***
Would you say positive things about Company X to other people?		LOY	−.928***
Would you recommend Company X to friends, neighbors and relatives?		LOY	−.971***
Are you satisfied with the way Company X communicates with you?		SAT	.701***
Are you, in general, satisfied with Company X?		SAT	.823***
Is Company X a quality company?		SAT	.854***

Significance level: *** .000

Figure 10.19 Exercise I.

Model Fit Summary

CMIN

Model	NPAR	CMIN	DF	P	CMIN/DF
Default model	20	70.018	25	.000	2.801
Saturated model	45	.000	0		
Independence model	9	1521.735	36	.000	42.270

RMR, GFI

Model	RMR	GFI	AGFI	PGFI
Default model	.116	.936	.885	.520
Saturated model	.000	1.000		
Independence model	1.315	.277	.096	.221

Baseline Comparisons

Model	NFI Delta1	RFI rho1	IFI Delta2	TLI rho2	CFI
Default model	.954	.934	.970	.956	.970
Saturated model	1.000		1.000		1.000
Independence model	.000	.000	.000	.000	.000

Parsimony-Adjusted Measures

Model	PRATIO	PNFI	PCFI
Default model	.694	.662	.673
Saturated model	.000	.000	.000
Independence model	1.000	.000	.000

NCP

Model	NCP	LO 90	HI 90
Default model	45.018	23.797	73.886
Saturated model	.000	.000	.000

Figure 10.20 Exercise II.

Model	NCP	LO 90	HI 90
Independence model	1485.735	1361.809	1617.033

FMIN

Model	FMIN	F0	LO 90	HI 90
Default model	.303	.195	.103	.320
Saturated model	.000	.000	.000	.000
Independence model	6.588	6.432	5.895	7.000

RMSEA

Model	RMSEA	LO 90	HI 90	PCLOSE
Default model	.088	.064	.113	.006
Independence model	.423	.405	.441	.000

AIC

Model	AIC	BCC	BIC	CAIC
Default model	110.018	111.828	178.953	198.953
Saturated model	90.000	94.072	245.103	290.103
Independence model	1539.735	1540.550	1570.756	1579.756

ECVI

Model	ECVI	LO 90	HI 90	MECVI
Default model	.476	.384	.601	.484
Saturated model	.390	.390	.390	.407
Independence model	6.666	6.129	7.234	6.669

HOELTER

Model	HOELTER .05	HOELTER .01
Default model	125	147
Independence model	8	9

Figure 10.20 (Continued)

Market insight

Marketing research has been investigating several relevant constructs in consumer behavior. One central concern is customer loyalty, the establishment of a long-term relationship with the customer. Among possible drivers of loyalty, marketing theory suggests the following: product quality, perceived value, satisfaction, switching costs, and trust.

1 Consider the sector in which the company you work for operates. What are relevant constructs to increase loyalty in your sector? Propose a SEM to measure the relationships.
2 What could be relevant indicators for each construct?
3 What is in your opinion the most important construct to achieve loyalty?

Suggested readings

Bagozzi, R. P., & Yi, Y. (2012). Specification, evaluation, and interpretation of structural equation models. *Journal of the Academy of Marketing Science, 40*(1), 8–34.

Bian, Q., & Forsythe, S. (2012). Purchase intention for luxury brands: A cross cultural comparison. *Journal of Business Research, 65*(10), 1443–1451.

Griffin, M., Babin, B. J., & Modianos, D. (2000). Shopping values of Russian consumers: The impact of habituation in a developing economy. *Journal of Retailing, 76*(1), 33–52.

Kim, Y. H., Lee, M. Y., & Kim, Y. K. (2011). A new shopper typology: Utilitarian and hedonic perspectives. *Journal of Global Academy of Marketing, 21*(2), 102–113.

Sharma, P., & Chan, R. (2015). Demystifying deliberate counterfeit purchase behaviour: Towards a unified conceptual framework. *Marketing Intelligence and Planning, 34*(3), 318–335.

Strizhakova, Y., Coulter, R. A., & Price, L. L. (2008). Branded products as a passport to global citizenship: Perspectives from developed and developing countries. *Journal of International Marketing, 16*(4), 57–85.

Vigneron, F., & Johnson, L. W. (2004). Measuring perceptions of brand luxury. *Journal of Brand Management, 11*(6), 484–506.

Appendix 1

Fitness center questionnaire

This questionnaire is part of a research that aims to identify which are the most common service failures in fitness centers, how fitness centers handle complaints, and what the customer satisfaction with the complaint handling is. Please rate the statements below by marking from (1) totally disagree to (7) totally agree. Thank you for your participation.

	Item
	Complaint Management Satisfaction
cs1	In general terms, I was satisfied with the complaint handling.
cs2	I was satisfied with the compensation I received.
cs3	I was pleased with the way I was treated.
cs4	I was satisfied with complaint handling system.
	Failure Severity
fs1	The failure made me deeply irritated.
fs2	The failure left me disappointed.
fs3	The failure caused me financial problems.
fs4	The failure caused me health damage.
fs4	My daily life was hampered due to failure.
	Interactional Justice
ij1	They appear to be telling the truth.
ij2	I was given a reasonable account as to why the original problem occurred.
ij3	They seemed very concerned about my problem.
ij4	I felt I was treated kindly.
ij5	They put a lot of positive energy into handling my problem.
	Procedural Justice
pj1	I have had an answer to my complaint.
pj2	It was easy to figure who to complain to in this organization.
pj3	They responded quickly to my complaint.
pj4	I was given an opportunity to tell my side of the story.
pj5	They were willing to adapt their complaint handling procedures to satisfy my needs.

	Distributive Justice
dj1	I got what I deserved from the complaint.
dj2	Given the circumstances, I feel that the retailer offered adequate compensation.
dj3	Taking everything into consideration, the manager's offer was quite fair.
dj4	The compensation met my expectations.
	Switching Intention
si1	I'm inclined to switch my fitness center.
si2	I've been looking for information about other fitness centers.
si3	After the failure, my desire to switch my fitness center increased.
si4	I'll certainly switch gyms.

What kind of failure happened? (In case of more than one fault, please choose the most serious one).

1   Defective equipment
2   Reduced number of equipment
3   Lack of attention on the part of the instructor
4   Wrong guidance from the instructor
5   Infrastructure problems (bathrooms, cleaning, air conditioning, swimming pool, etc.)

How did you complain? (In case of more than one medium, please choose the one that you used the most).

1   Personally
2   By email
3   By WhatsApp
4   I put the complaint in a complaint box
5   On social media

I am

1   Male
2   Female

What is your marital status?

1   Single
2   Living with partner, no children
3   Living with partner, with children
4   Other

What is your monthly income, before tax?

1   Less than $ 2,000,00
2   $ 2,000,00 – $ 5,000.00

3    $ 5,000.00 – $ 10,000,00
4   More than $ 10,000.00

What is the highest degree or level of education you have completed?

1   Elementary school
2   High school
3   Bachelor's degree
4   Master's degree or higher

Follow-up

After three to four months, a follow-up was done to check the customers' reactions. In the follow-up, respondents were classified in two groups:

1   Permanence: the respondent remained customer
2   Defection: the respondent stopped his subscription at the fitness center.

Appendix 2

Supermarket questionnaire

This questionnaire is part of a research to evaluate the important attributes driving customers' choice for a supermarket. Please rate the attributes below, by marking from (1) not important through (7) very important. Thank you for your participation.

v1	distance
v2	product variety
v3	internal look
v4	fast checkout
v5	advertising
v6	price
v7	easy access
v8	product quality
v9	product layout
v10	helpful staff
v11	special promotion
v12	credit card
v13	parking lot
v14	product availability
v15	comfortable store
v16	customer service at specific department (bakery, meat, deli)
v17	loyalty program
v18	pre-paid check
v19	external look
v20	restroom
v21	delivery
v22	convenience store
v23	store card
v24	nearby convenience stores
v25	special equipment
v26	baggers

v1	distance
v27	store buying habit
v28	notebook notation
v29	complaints handling
v30	perishable products' quality
v31	opening hours
v32	lowest price guarantee (financial refund if cheaper product is found)
v33	online/phone purchase
v34	safety place
v35	repurchase intention

I am:

1   Male
2   Female
3   Other

What is your age?

1   < 25
2   26–40
3   41–60
4   > 60

What is your monthly family income, before tax?

1   Less than $1,200
2   $1,201–$2,400
3   $2,401–$4,800
4   more than $4,800

What is the distance (in km) from your home to the supermarket?

1   Up to 2 km
2   2 to 4 km
3   4 to 6 km
4   more than 6 km

How do you go to the store most often?

1   Car
2   Taxi
3   Bus
4   Walking
5   Other

How often do you go to the supermarket?

1   Daily
2   Once or twice per week
3   Every two weeks
4   Once per month
5   Other

Type of neighborhood

Respondents in the survey were categorized based on the type of neighborhood where they live. Type has three categories:

1   High-income neighborhood
2   Middle-income neighborhood
3   Low-income neighborhood

Bibliography

Aaker, J. L. (1997). Dimensions of brand personality. *Journal of Marketing Research, 34*(3), 347–356.

Anderson, R. E., & Srinivasan, S. S. (2003). E-satisfaction and e-loyalty: A contingency framework. *Psychology & Marketing, 20*(2), 123–138.

Bagozzi, R. P., & Yi, Y. (2012). Specification, evaluation, and interpretation of structural equation models. *Journal of the Academy of Marketing Science, 40*(1), 8–34.

Bagozzi, R. P., Yi, Y., & Philips, L. W. (1991, Sept). Assessing construct validity in organizational research. *Administrative Science Quarterly, 36*(3), 421–458.

Bhattacharjee, A., & Mogilner, C. (2014). Happiness from ordinary and extraordinary experiences. *Journal of Consumer Research, 41*(1), 1–17.

Bian, Q., & Forsythe, S. (2012). Purchase intention for luxury brands: A cross cultural comparison. *Journal of Business Research, 65*(10), 1443–1451.

Bowen, J. (1990). Development of a taxonomy of services to gain strategic marketing insights. *Journal of the Academy of Marketing Science, 18*(1), 43–49.

Box, G. E., Jenkins, G. M., & Reinsel, G. C. (1994). *Time series analysis: Forecasting and control*. John Wiley & Sons.

Caprariello, P. A., & Reis, H. T. (2013). To do, to have, or to share? Valuing experiences over material possessions depends on the involvement of others. *Journal of Personality and Social Psychology, 104*(2), 199.

Capraro, A. J., Broniarczyk, S., & Srivastava, R. K. (2003). Factors influencing the likelihood of customer defection: The role of consumer knowledge. *Journal of the Academy of Marketing Science, 31*(2), 164–175.

Colgate, M., & Lang, B. (2001). Switching barriers in consumer markets: An investigation of the financial services industry. *Journal of Consumer Marketing, 18*(4), 332–347.

Damodar, N. Gujarati (2004). *Basic econometrics*. The Mc-Graw Hill.

Fornell, C., Johnson, M. D., Anderson, E. W., Cha, J., & Bryant, B. E. (1996). The American customer satisfaction index: Nature, purpose, and findings. *Journal of Marketing, 60*(4), 7–18.

Furse, D. H., Punj, G. N., & Stewart, D. W. (1984). A typology of individual search strategies among purchasers of new automobiles. *Journal of Consumer Research, 10*(4), 417–431.

Griffin, M., Babin, B. J., & Modianos, D. (2000). Shopping values of Russian consumers: The impact of habituation in a developing economy. *Journal of Retailing, 76*(1), 33–52.

Hair, J. F., Anderson, R. E., Tatham, R. L., & Black, W. C. (2005). *Multivariate data analysis* (6th ed.). New Jersey.

Hershberger, S. L., Molenaar, P. C., & Corneal, S. E. (1996). *A hierarchy of univariate and multivariate structural time series models. Advanced structural equation modeling: Issues and techniques* (pp. 159–194).

Hirschman, E. C. (1979). Differences in consumer purchase behavior by credit card payment system. *Journal of Consumer Research, 6*(1), 58–66.

Hsee, C. K., Yang, Y., Li, N., & Shen, L. (2009). Wealth, warmth, and well-being: Whether happiness is relative or absolute depends on whether it is about money, acquisition, or consumption. *Journal of Marketing Research, 46*(3), 396–409.

Huang, M. H., & Yu, S. (1999). Are consumers inherently or situationally brand loyal? A set inter-correlation account for conscious brand loyalty and nonconscious inertia. *Psychology & Marketing, 16*(6), 523–544.

Huang, P., Lurie, N. H., & Mitra, S. (2009). Searching for experience on the web: An empirical examination of consumer behavior for search and experience goods. *Journal of marketing, 73*(2), 55–69.

Johnston, J. (1972). *Econometric Methods*. McGraw Hill.

Jones, M. A., Mothersbaugh, D. L., & Beatty, S. E. (2000). Switching barriers and repurchase intentions in services. *Journal of Retailing, 76*(2), 259–274.

Kim, J. C., Park, B., & Dubois, D. (2018). How consumers' political ideology and status-maintenance goals interact to shape their desire for luxury goods. *Journal of Marketing, 82*(6), 132–149.

Kim, Y. H., Lee, M. Y., & Kim, Y. K. (2011). A new shopper typology: Utilitarian and hedonic perspectives. *Journal of Global Academy of Marketing, 21*(2), 102–113.

Kmenta, J. (1997). *Elements of Econometrics*. University of Michigan Press.

Leng, C. Y., & Botelho, D. (2010). How does national culture impact on consumers decision-making styles? A cross cultural study in Brazil, the United States and Japan. *BAR–Brazilian Administration Review, 7*(3), 260–275.

Maroco, J. (2003). *Análise de Equações Estruturais: Fundamentos teóricos, software e aplicações*. Pêro Pinheiro (PT): Report Number.

Morgan, R. M., & Hunt, S. D. (1994). The commitment-trust theory of relationship marketing. *Journal of Marketing, 58*(3), 20–38.

Nicolao, L., Irwin, J. R., & Goodman, J. K. (2009). Happiness for sale: Do experiential purchases make consumers happier than material purchases? *Journal of Consumer Research, 36*(2), 188–198.

Papadopoulos, N., Martín, O. M., Cleveland, M., & Laroche, M. (2011). Identity, demographics, and consumer behaviors. *International Marketing Review, 28*(3), 244–266.

Richins, M. L. (1997). Measuring emotions in the consumption experience. *Journal of Consumer Research, 24*(2), 127–146.

Santonen, T. (2007). Price sensitivity as an indicator of customer defection in retail banking. *International Journal of Bank Marketing, 25*(1), 39–55.

Sharma, P., & Chan, R. (2015). Demystifying deliberate counterfeit purchase behaviour: Towards a unified conceptual framework. *Marketing Intelligence and Planning, 34*(3), 318–335.

Sharma, S. (1996). *Applied multivariate techniques*. John Wiley & Sons.

Singh, J. (1990). A typology of consumer dissatisfaction response styles. *Journal of Retailing, 66*(1), 57.

Strizhakova, Y., Coulter, R. A., & Price, L. L. (2008). Branded products as a passport to global citizenship: Perspectives from developed and developing countries. *Journal of International Marketing, 16*(4), 57–85.

Tabachnick, B. E, & Fidel, L. S. (1996). *Using multivariate statistics*. Allyn & Bacon.

Tabachnick, B. G., & Fidell, L. S. (2006). *Chapter 18: Time series analysis. Using multivariate statistics* (5th ed.). Pearson International Edition. Retrieved March 16 2021, from https://media.pearson-cmg.com/ab/ab_tabachnick_multistats_6/datafiles/M18_TABA9574_06_SE_C18.pdf

Trubik, E., & Smith, M. (2000). Developing a model of customer defection in the Australian banking industry. *Managerial Auditing Journal, 15*(5), 199–208.

Vigneron, F., & Johnson, L. W. (2004). Measuring perceptions of brand luxury. *Journal of Brand Management, 11*(6), 484–506.

Wu, L. W. (2011). Satisfaction, inertia, and customer loyalty in the varying levels of the zone of tolerance and alternative attractiveness. *Journal of Services Marketing, 25*(5), 310–322.

Zampetakis, L. A. (2014). The emotional dimension of the consumption of luxury counterfeit goods: An empirical taxonomy. *Marketing Intelligence & Planning, 32*(1), 21–40.

Zeelenberg, M., & Pieters, R. (2004). Beyond valence in customer dissatisfaction: A review and new findings on behavioral responses to regret and disappointment in failed services. *Journal of Business Research, 57*(4), 445–455.

Index

For Product Safety Concerns and Information please contact our EU
representative GPSR@taylorandfrancis.com
Taylor & Francis Verlag GmbH, Kaufingerstraße 24, 80331 München, Germany

* 9 781032 052199 *